FAT QUARTERS

FAT QUARTERS

Small Fabrics, More Than

50 BIG IDEAS

LARK
New York

New York

An Imprint of Sterling Publishing
1166 Avenue of the Americas
New York, NY 10036

ISBN 978-1-4549-0879-7

Distributed in Canada by Sterling Publishing
c/o Canadian Manda Group, 664 Annette Street
Toronto, Ontario, Canada M6S 2C8
Distributed in the United Kingdom by GMC Distribution Services
Castle Place, 166 High Street, Lewes, East Sussex, England BN7 1XU
Distributed in Australia by Capricorn Link (Australia) Pty. Ltd.
P.O. Box 704, Windsor, NSW 2756, Australia

For information about custom editions, special sales, and premium and corporate purchases,
please contact Sterling Special Sales at 800-805-5489 or specialsales@sterlingpublishing.com.

Manufactured in China

2 4 6 8 10 9 7 5 3 1

larkcrafts.com

CONTENTS

WELCOME!

Whether you're a fat quarter enthusiast by choice, or a fat quarter collector because you just can't help yourself when you see great-looking fabric, there's a good chance that you've got some of these lovely bits of material languishing in your stash, waiting for the perfect project to come along. And you're in good company: fat quarters are wonderfully (and woefully!) easy to collect. But, as you've probably discovered, they are much harder to actually use. Join us as an incredibly talented group of designers and I show you what we've made using fat quarters.

HOW FAR CAN A FAT QUARTER 18 X 22 INCHES (45.7 X 55.9 CM) OF FABRIC GET YOU?

We've assembled 52 projects that answer that question. There are so many great things to make for yourself, to give as gifts, to share with wee ones, to cozy up your life, and to decorate your space. Be sure to look at the How to Cut a Quarter section (page 1) because there are also terrific ways to cut fat quarters into practical shapes and sizes that will make them incredibly useful to you.

GETTING STARTED

MATERIALS AND TOOLS
You only need a few simple supplies and materials to make the projects in this book.

FAT QUARTERS
The wee (but mighty!) fat quarter is easy to love and to collect. Although there are slight variations in the sizes of fat quarters, for the purposes of this book, we consider the fat quarter to be 18 x 22 inches (45.7 x 55.9 cm) of hoardable fabric goodness.

A fat quarter is essentially a half yard of quilting cotton cut in half, which is much more usable than its ¼ yard (22.9 cm) counterpart (9 x 44 inches [22.9 x 111.8 cm]). And mighty is the fat quarter. Used as a whole piece or cut into little bits, there's a lot you can do with fat quarters. To be exact, you'll find 52 great project here. Take a look at the How to Cut a Quarter section for some ideas on how to cut fat quarters into all kinds of usable pieces.

You'll be amazed at how far your fat quarters can go! And when you've finally used some fat quarters from your stash, you'll be delighted with what you've created. And soon it will be time to buy even more fat quarters!

Make these beauties with . . .

HOW MANY FAT QUARTERS DO I NEED FOR A PROJECT?

1 single, special fat quarter:
- Patchwork Tie (page 124)
- Pieced Pocket Tote (page 63)
- Ruffle-Embellished Sweater (page 121)
- FQ Flower Trio (page 132)

2 coordinating quarters:
- Boho Bag (page 53)
- Floppy Animal Friends (page 30)

- Child's FQ Reversible Apron (page 13)
- Quilted Frame (page 99)
- Mushroom Tote (page 37)

3 or more fat quarters or scraps of fat quarters:
- Rainbow Chevron Skirt (page 119)
- Patchwork Picnic Blanket (page 95)
- Hoop Tree (page 101)
- Cross Roads Lap Quilt (page 89)
- Chevron Curtains (page 105)

HOW TO CUT A QUARTER
Many patchwork and quilting projects call for squares. How many squares can you get from a fat quarter? The answer may surprise you!

- 99 2-inch (5.1 cm) squares
- 56 2½-inch (6.4 cm) squares
- 42 3-inch (7.6 cm) squares
- 30 3½-inch (8.9 cm) squares
- 20 4-inch (10.2 cm) squares
- 16 4½-inch (11.4 cm) squares
- 12 5-inch (12.7 cm) squares
- 12 5½-inch (14 cm) squares
- 9 6-inch (15.2 cm) squares
- 6 6½-inch (16.5 cm) squares

And that's just the beginning! Need some rectangles? How about four 4 x 22-inch (10.2 x 55.9 cm) strips? Or six 3 x 22-inch (7.6 x 55.9 cm) sections? Or nine 2 x 22-inch (5.1 x 55.9 cm) strips for binding? If you piece end to end, that's almost 200 inches (5.1 m) of pretty binding from a single fat quarter. See? Fat quarters are mighty flexible.

OTHER SUPPLIES & TOOLS

The fat quarter is the star of this show, but you'll likely need a few other supplies to create the projects in this book including quilt batting, fusible webbing, fusible fleece, trims like rickrack and pompoms, embroidery floss, and sewing thread in all kinds of glorious colors.

BASIC SEWING KIT

- Flexible measuring tape
- 2 pairs of scissors: one for cutting paper, one for cutting fabric
- Small embroidery scissors
- Sewing machine and needles [specific needles and other equipment may be listed in Materials]
- Straight pins
- Needles for hand sewing and embroidery
- Seam ripper
- Thread
- Marking tools (disappearing fabric marker, washable fabric marker, chalk)
- Iron and ironing board
- Turning tool
- Pencil
- Rotary cutter, mat, and ruler (optional)

DON'T FORGET THE GEAR!

You'll need a sewing machine, an iron and ironing board, a variety of hand-sewing needles, a ruler, a rotary cutter and mat, and a few pairs of scissors to create most of the projects in this book, with a few specialty tools here and there. See page 2 for the Basic Sewing Kit you'll need for most projects in this book.

SPECIAL TECHNIQUES

The vast majority of the projects in this book use very basic sewing techniques. If you've ever sewn an apron or a pillow or a potholder, you're all set.

While there's nothing too sophisticated here, there are a few techniques and terms you'll need to know. A few sewing or quilting techniques may be new to you, so here's a brief survey of them . . . and then on to the fun!

USING TEMPLATES

A template is a pattern shape cut from stiff paper that you trace onto fabric. In the back of the book, you'll find all the templates you need to make the fabulous projects.

Enlarge each template based on the percentage given with the instructions. Then follow the individual project instructions for using the templates as well as for cutting out the additional parts and pieces you'll need for your project.

BASTING

Basting is stitching that is easy-to-remove and temporary. You baste to hold fabric in place until you are ready to do final sewing. To baste, use a longer stitch length on your sewing machine or stitch by hand using a long running stitch. Basting is particularly helpful with English paper piecing: In this process, you fold over and then baste the edges of shapes to their paper templates. Remove the basting stitches (and the templates) later when you have completed the final sewing.

TOPSTITCHING

Sometimes functional and sometimes purely decorative, topstitching means sewing with the top of your project facing up. Keep in mind that this stitching will be visible when the project is complete, so attractive top stitching is perfect when you need a simple, finished edge.

APPLIQUÉ

Appliqué is the process of permanently attaching one piece of material to the top of another, usually by stitching. The projects in *Fat Quarters* use a variety of appliqué methods, from turned-edge appliqué to raw-edge appliqué. While there are other kinds of appliqué, many of the projects in this book use paper-backed fusible web to attach fabric shapes on top of other fabric.

The process of using fusible web is super simple: Trace your appliqué template onto the paper backing of the fusible web (flipping it if necessary), iron the webbing to the back of the fabric. Cut out the shape and remove the backing. Finally, iron the fabric shape in place wherever you'd like it to go.

If you're not turning under your fabric edges, you've got options for how to finish them. (1) Create a simple stitched line just inside of the appliqué shape (and leave the edges raw), (2) zigzag stitch over the edge with your machine, or (3) embroider a decorative stitch over the edges to seal them. Use a blanket stitch or another decorative stitch.

EMBROIDERY

Embroidery is decorative topstitching. It's usually done with cotton floss in a pretty color or silk embroidery floss. Embroidery provides a warm, handmade, personal touch to an item. Combine embroidery with a precious fat quarter, and you've got pure magic.

To get started with your embroidery, you'll need to enlarge and then transfer the embroidery motif provided to fabric.

For light fabrics

1. Tape the motif to a sunny window pane.

2. Tape your fabric in place over the motif.

3. Trace the pattern through to the fabric with a pencil or a water soluble marker.

For dark fabrics

1. Trace the motif onto tissue paper.

2. Pin the tissue paper to the fabric.

3. Stitch through the paper and the fabric.

4. Remove the paper later.

There's nothing too scientific here in terms of stitchery; you only need to use simple stitches. See the chart on page 5 for a refresher.

HANDY STITCH ILLUSTRATIONS

Blanket Stitch

Cross-Stitch

Satin Stitch

French Knot

Running Stitch

Ladder Stitch

Backstitch

Split stitch

Whipstitch

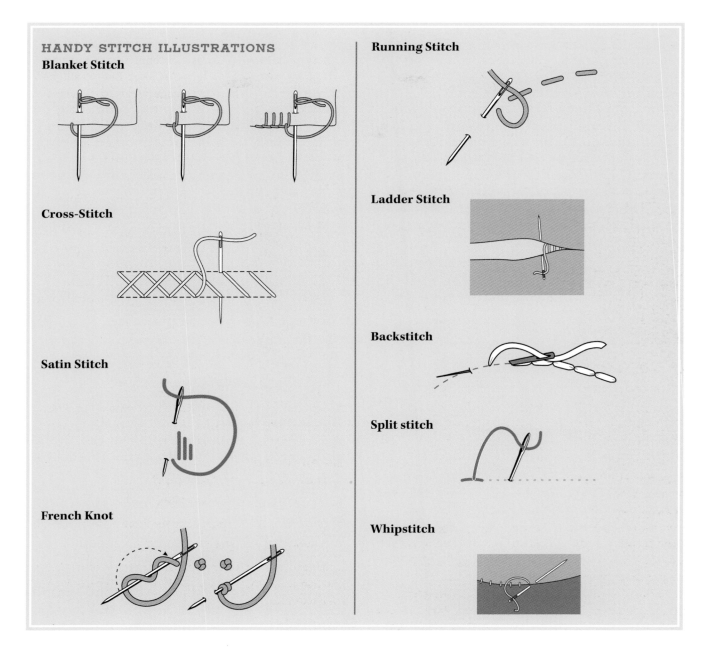

BOXED CORNERS

Boxed corners are a quick and easy way to provide depth and function to an item. Several projects in this book—primarily bags and baskets used for storage—use boxed corners. And they are easy to make.

After you've joined two pieces of fabric, either with two side seams or seams along the left, bottom, and right edges and with right sides together, fold the corners flat onto themselves to create a flat point, matching the side and bottom and seams. Measure in from the point (from the seam allowance, not the edge of the fabric) to the recommended measurement and draw a line with a fabric marker (see Figure 1). Stitch along the line and then trim the seam allowance to ¼ inch (6 mm) (see Figure 2).

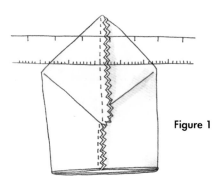

Figure 1

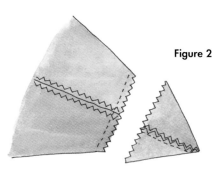

Figure 2

PIECING PATCHWORK & QUILTING

Because fat quarters are a natural pick for patchwork and quilting projects, you'll find a good numbers of these projects in this book.

Piecing

For the projects that use patchwork, you'll need to first piece—or sew—your cut fabric shapes together. Essentially, you pin one piece of fabric to the other, right sides facing. Run them through your sewing machine about ¼ inch from the edge of the fabric.. Then press the seams to one side or another, based on the project instructions. For more intricate patterns, things can get more involved.

Foundation Paper Piecing

In some cases, particularly when you are piecing an intricate pattern, you'll find it a lot easier to sew your fabric pieces to paper layers before you begin to piece them. This is a lot easier than struggling to manipulate itsy bitsy pieces of fabric. Called foundation paper piecing, the paper backing gives fabric enough body to make it much easier to handle.

1. First, transfer your template to paper; enlarging it if needed.

NOTE: When you are piecing small pieces of fabric, shorten the stitch length on your sewing machine. This makes it easier to remove the paper backing in the last step.

2. Follow the project instructions or use the paper-piecing pattern as a guide to cut rough shapes from your fabrics, adding plenty of extra room—at least ½ inch (2.5 cm)—to each edge.

3. Starting with section 1 and working your way numerically around the pattern, place the printed side of the pattern face down. Place your section 1 fabric piece on the back of the paper, right side up. Glue it in place with a dab of glue stick if necessary. Trim around the fabric piece to create a ¼-inch (6 mm) seam allowance, using the pattern lines as a guide.

NOTE: Always sew on the printed side of the paper and lay fabric pieces down on the back.

4. Place your section 2 fabric piece on your section 1 fabric piece, right sides together, with the raw edge matching. Hold or pin this piece in place. Turn the paper over, and stitch along the line between them. Turn your paper back over, fold the section 2 fabric over flat (so both sections are right sides up), and iron the fabrics. Continue working your way around the template with each of the sections.

5. Gently remove the paper backing and follow the rest of the project instructions.

English Paper Piecing

Have you seen those perfect little hexagon appliqués and wondered how to create such neat and tidy turned edges? English paper piecing is the answer. Use this technique to create appliqué shapes (like for the Sweet Dreams Toddler Sheets, page 17) or for shapes that are then stitched together, edge to edge, to create "fabric."

1. First, enlarge or copy the specified number of paper templates and cut them out.

2. Pin the template to the back of a small piece of fabric and cut around the template, leaving a ¼-inch (6 mm) seam allowance on all sides.

3. Fold the seam allowance over the edges of the template and stitch the seam allowance in place with long basting stitches (see Figure 3).

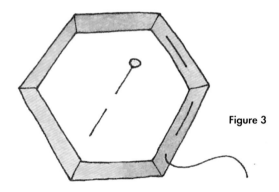

Figure 3

4. Press the shapes.

5. Stitch the hexagons to each other (for patchwork) or to a base fabric (for appliqué, as in this illustration). Use a whipstitch, gently removing the templates and the basting stitches before you attach all the sides (see Figure 4).

Figure 4

Quilt Sandwich

After you've pieced your top layer together—but before you do the actual quilting stitches on your patchwork or appliqué quilt project—you must layer and secure the three quilt parts together. This is called making a quilt sandwich. Essentially, you stack the layers: (1) place the quilt backing on the bottom, face down; (2) smooth the batting over this fabric, and (3) place the quilt top, face up, atop the two layers. (4) Smooth out the wrinkles with your hand as well as possible. Be sure the edges of each layer are lined up with each other (see Figure 5).

Figure 5

Next, before you begin to do your final quilt stitching, you'll need to secure together the three layers of your quilt. Use either long basting stitches, pins, or spray.

Quilting

Once you've secured your layers together, you, crafty friend, are ready to stitch your patchwork or quilt layers together. And you have options here, too, depending on the finished look you'd like to achieve:

Straight-line quilting is used to create straight horizontal or vertical lines or to create a grid, as in the All My Heart Mini Quilt (page 85). Simply stitch straight lines across your pieced patchwork or quilt top, rolling your quilt edges for better access if needed (see Figure 6). A quilting bar attachment, which helps you create evenly spaced lines, can come in handy for this process.

Figure 6

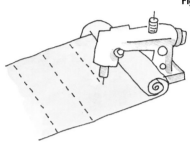

Stitch in the Ditch quilting is a process in which you stitch into the seams created by your patchwork piecing. With this method, your stitch lines become invisible (see Figure 7).

Figure 7

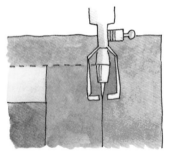

Free-motion quilting has a freeform, sketchy look, perfectly showcased in the Groovy Vibes Quilt (page 75). Simply drop your feed dogs, attach a quilting or darning foot, and guide the fabric through the sewing machine with your hands, moving in multiple directions, to create continuous lines of stitching (see Figure 8). A common method is to create a meandering line of stitches, also called stippling.

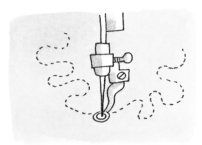

Figure 8

Binding

Binding is time-consuming but it serves a worthwhile purpose. The addition of binding tape finishes the edges on quilts and patchwork projects so they don't fray or unravel. Crafters are divided on how they feel about the process. Some people love this part of finishing, and some people could do without it. Either way, the addition of binding is essential. Besides, it often adds a pretty pop of color to your project!

What follows are the basic binding steps, including info on dealing with corners. If you're binding a project with rounded corners or a circular object, like the Circle Hot Pot Pads (page 137), you don't have to worry about corners. The steps below will be the same for starting, joining the ends, and wrapping to the back. Take a deep breath: you can do this!

1. After you've quilted the layers together, lay your project flat and trim the layers so they're all the same size.

2. Starting midway on one edge or near a corner, pin and then stitch the right side of the binding to the right side of the fabric (see Figure 9), folding over the starting edge. Use the seam allowance in the instructions.

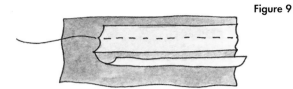

Figure 9

NOTE: If you'd like to join your binding ends, don't fold over the starting edge; instead, leave yourself plenty of extra unstitched binding at your starting place. When you get back around to your start (step 5), bring the binding ends together to decide how much binding you'll need and to decide where to place the seam: mark or pin at the designated spot. Unfold both ends, place them together, right sides facing, and stitch them together at your mark. Continue attaching the binding and proceed to step 6.

3. Stop stitching as you approach the first corner and clip the threads to remove the project from the machine. Fold the binding straight up over itself to form a 45° angle at the corner (see Figure 10).

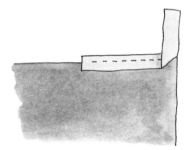

Figure 10

4. Fold the binding straight down to make it even with the next edge and continue pinning and stitching the binding in place (see Figure 11 on page 10). Continue working your way around the edges, using the same process for any additional corners.

Figure 11

5. When you near your starting point, stitch your binding strip over the folded-over starting edge of the binding.

6. Fold the binding over the edges (not too tightly) to the back. Pull the edge of the binding just over the seam line that attached the binding (the one you just stitched) and pin it in place. Create diagonal folds at the corners and pin them in place.

7. Working from the back, use a slipstitch to attach the binding (see Figure 12). Working from the front, stitch in the ditch.

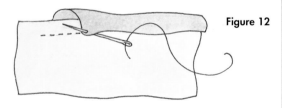

Figure 12

Making Your Own Binding

Binding strips are available prepackaged in stores but homemade (in a fave fabric) and pieced binding really sets my heart aflutter. It's an easy process, even easier if you have a bias tape maker, probably my favorite craft tool of all time. Here's how to do it:

1. Determine how much binding you'll need. In most cases, the project instructions will provide this information. If not, simply measure or add together the lengths of the edges you're binding, plus 4 to 6 inches (10.2 to 15.2 cm) extra.

2. Cut a strip of fabric to the recommended width in the project instructions (or to the required width for your bias tape maker).

Connect strips to create the length you need by pinning and stitching the short ends together, with the right sides facing. Stitch along the short end (see Figure 13). Press the seams open.

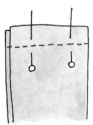

Figure 13

For less bulk in your binding, and especially if you're working with strips of the same fabric, pin the short ends together at a right angle, with right sides facing, and stitch diagonally across the corner (see Figure 14). Press the seams open.

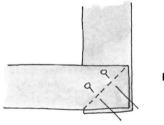

Figure 14

3. Turn under each long side edge to the recommended amount and then press the binding in half. Or pull your strip through the bias tape maker (which makes the side folds for you) and press. Then press the binding in half. Ta da!

Now it's time to gather some fat quarters and get started with the fun projects that follow.

BABIES
& KIDS

FINISHED SIZE
- 17 x 20½ inches (43.2 x 52.1 cm)

MATERIALS
- 2 fat quarters
- Basic Sewing Kit (page 2)
- Template (page 147)
- Thread to match the fabrics
- 12 inches (30.5 cm) of rickrack trim
- 18 inches (45.7 cm) of pom-pom trim
- Zipper foot (optional)
- 2 yards (1.8 m) of grosgrain ribbon, 1 inch (2.5 cm) wide
- 1 button, 1 or 1¾ inches (2.5 or 4.4 cm) in diameter
- NOTE: *Check the direction of your fabric print. If it runs in a specific direction, to be sure the pattern is oriented to run the length of the fat quarter, or buy ¾ yard (68.6 cm) in a traditional cut to be certain you have enough length either parallel or perpendicular to the selvedge.*

CHILD'S FQ REVERSIBLE APRON

DESIGN BY ANNELIESE

Stitch this double-sided apron, make a mess, turn . . . and repeat. Add rickrack and pompom trim to make the apron as pretty as it can be.

INSTRUCTIONS

1. Fold a fat quarter in half lengthwise (it should measure 9 x 22 inches [22.9 x 55.9 cm]). Position the Armhole template with the straight edges aligned with the top and side of the fabric (not the fold). Cut two armhole pieces this way from each fat quarter; you'll use these pieces to make the pockets. You'll have four triangular pieces for making two pockets; the remaining fat quarters (minus armholes) are the apron pieces (see Figure 1).

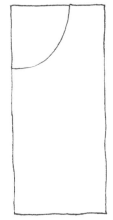

Figure 1

2. Matching the edge of the rickrack and the fabric, baste a piece of rickrack along the top curve of one of

each of the two armhole/pocket pieces. Baste down the center of the rickrack.

3. Pin two pocket pieces together with right sides facing and stitch around using a ⅜-inch (9.5 mm) seam allowance Be sure to leave a 2-inch (5.1 cm) opening in one of the straight sides for turning.

Note: You may need to adjust your seam allowance along the top curve of the pocket so that the stitching is aligned with the basting stitches that run along the center of the rickrack. This way the rickrack will be perfectly positioned.

4. Clip your corners and turn right side out. Press, being careful to tuck

in the raw edges where you left the gap for turning.

5. Position the pocket on the center of the apron piece, about 3 inches (7.6 cm) below the bottom of the armholes. Pin and stitch in place along the straight sides as close as possible to the edge of the pocket. Repeat for second pocket piece.

6. Baste the pom-pom trim along the bottom of one of the apron pieces. Place the trim so the pom-poms are facing up away from the hem. (After you sew the two apron pieces together and turn the apron right side out, the pom-poms will hang down from the hem.)

Note: It's a matter of personal taste, but I like a bit of the webbing to show; you could, however, use a zipper foot and sew closer to the pom-poms so that they dangle from the hem.

7. Cut two pieces of ribbon 21 inches (53.3 cm) long for the apron ties, and one piece 16 inches (40.6 cm) long for the neck. Turn under one raw end on each of the pieces twice (turn under ¼ of an inch [6 mm] and turn under ¼ of an inch [6 mm] again). Zigzag or straight-stitch down the fabric to prevent it from fraying.

8. Baste the raw edges of the two 21-inch pieces (53.3 cm) of ribbon to the sides of the apron ⅜ inch (9.5 mm) below the armholes. Align the edge of the ribbon with the raw edge of the fabric so the ribbon is lying toward the center of the apron.

9. Place the two apron pieces right sides together and pin around all the edges except for the top; leave that open for turning. Be careful to keep the ribbon ties and pom-pom trim out of the way. You'll have a bit of bulk along the hem depending on the size of your pom-poms.

10. Stitch around all sides (except for the top) using a ⅜-inch (9.5 mm) seam allowance. Clip the corners. Turn right side out and press well.

11. Turn the top raw edges of the apron in ⅜ inch (9.5 mm) and press. Tuck in the raw edge of the shorter ribbon on one side and pin in place.

12. Topstitch the top of the apron close to the folded edge, being sure to catch the raw edge of the ribbon.

13. Create a buttonhole large enough to fit the button in the right-hand corner of the top of your apron, opposite the neck ribbon. Open the buttonhole using scissors or a seam ripper.

14. Now sew the button to the ribbon about 1 inch (2.5 cm) from the finished edge, or try it on your child and find where it fits best. With just one button you can easily twist the ribbon to reverse the apron without the discomfort of another button on the wrong side of the apron. Enjoy!

FINISHED SIZE

- **Design on pillowcase: about 20½ x 6 inches (52.1 x 15.25 cm)**
- **Design on sheet: about 16½ x 4½ inches (41.9 x 11.4 cm)**

MATERIALS

- **A variety of fat quarters and scraps**
- **Basic Sewing Kit (page 2)**
- **1 cotton standard pillowcase and sheet**
- **Templates (page 147)**
- **Paper or cardstock**
- **Ruler (optional)**
- **Embroidery floss and sewing thread to match**
- **NOTE:** *Prewash your sheet and pillowcase to avoid undesired shrinkage later.*

SWEET DREAMS TODDLER SHEETS

Help your child transition to a toddler bed by covering the new bed with sheets decorated with wee hexies, a stitched message, and that special touch of hand-stitched applique.

DESIGN BY
NICOLE VOS VAN AVEZATHE

4 FAT Quarters

INSTRUCTIONS

1. Press the pillowcase and transfer the lettering to the pillowcase. Make sure the lettering is centered and at least 2¼ inches (5.7 cm) from the top of the pillowcase. (Assuming the pillowcase is going to be used, this leaves enough space for your child's head without Xs or hexagon shapes embossing themselves on his or her face the next morning.)

2. Use embroidery floss and a cross-stitch (page 5) for the letters. Work as neatly as you can, but don't worry too much about a little variation in your stitching. After you've finished, rinse the pillowcase to remove the markings.

3. Sort the fabric scraps by color. You can use various shades of one color or an array of colors. There should be enough variety so you can make gradual color or shade changes. Choose a light, contrasting shade for the heart of the flower. If you can fussy-cut a print, that's definitely a bonus!

4. Cut 31 paper hexagons from the ¾-inch (1.9 cm) template: 23 for the pillowcase and 8 for the sheet. Cut 7 paper hexagons from the 1-inch (2.5 cm) template: these will form the flower in the center of the sheet. Baste the edges of the hexagons (see Figure 1).

Figure 1

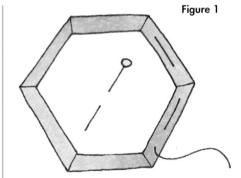

5. Arrange the hexagons on the far left and right of the pillow in a flower shape minus one hexagon (using the photo as a guide) and stitch them together with a whipstitch (page 5). Stitch to the pillowcase by hand as indicated (see Figure 2). When you reach the point that there's just one side of the hexagon left to stitch down to the background, it is time to remove the template. Carefully remove your basting stitches with a small scissor and gently pull the template out. Fold the seam allowance under and finish the stitching.

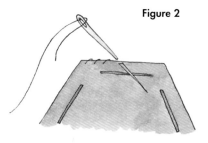

Figure 2

6. Rotate the "missing" petal slightly and stitch it onto the pillowcase. Arrange the rest of the hexagons in a playful way, keeping the gradual color change in mind, and stitch them to the pillowcase.

7. Press the sheet. When in use, the top of the sheet will be folded down, so that's where the flower should be added. Measure about 1¼ inches (3.2 cm) up from the bottom of the folded-down edge, center the 1-inch (2.5 cm) hexagons in a flower shape, and stitch them to the sheet by hand. Arrange the ¾-inch (1.9 cm) hexagons on either side of the flower, stitch them together as needed, and then appliqué them onto the sheet.

8. Sweet dreams!

TIP: I used a water-erasable marker to transfer the Xs to the pillowcase. If you choose this method of transferring, it is helpful to mark the height of the lettering onto the pillowcase by simply drawing lines with the water erasable pen and a ruler.

MATERIALS

- 3 fat quarters of coordinating fabrics: 1 of fabric A (front), 1 of fabric B (back), 1 of fabric C (front pocket)
- Basic Sewing Kit (page 2)
- 1 pillow form, 16 inches (40.6 cm)
- **NOTE:** *All seam allowances are ¼ inch (6 mm) unless otherwise indicated.*

CHILD'S TRAVEL PILLOW TOTE

By plane, train, or automobile, this all-in-one pillow tote is the perfect cozy companion for trips. It's a comfy headrest for a tired child. Plus it has an easy access pocket for tucking in a journal, tablet, pencils, or crafting supplies

DESIGN BY MEGAN HUNT

3 FAT Quarters

INSTRUCTIONS

1. Cut fabric as follows:

- One piece from fabric A, 20 x 17 inches (50.8 x 43.2 cm).
- One piece from fabric B, 20 x 17 inches (50.8 x 43.2 cm).
- One piece from fabric C, 17 x 10 inches (43.2 x 25.4 cm).
- Two pieces from fabric C for the straps, each 17 x 3½ inches (43.2 x 8.9 cm).

2. Fold one fabric C strap in half lengthwise, right sides together, and lightly press. Stitch the long side and turn it right side out. Press again with the seam centered in the back.

Repeat this for the second strap so you have two neat fabric strips.

3. Fold the top of fabric A down 2 inches (5.1 cm), wrong sides together, to make a 2-inch (5.1 cm) hem for the upper hem of the pillow. Stitch across the bottom edge of the folded fabric to secure. Repeat with fabric B to create the piece for the pillow back.

4. Attach one of the straps to the top of the pillow front. Measure 6 inches (15.2 cm) from each side of the top of the fabric and pin the strap in place, with the right side of the strap facing the wrong side of the front piece and the raw edges of the strap lined up with the hem edge from step 3. Sew in place

to secure the first strap. Repeat this step for the second strap and the pillow back.

5. With the fabric wrong side up, fold the long top edge of fabric C down 1½ inches (3.8 cm) to create the top edge of the pocket. Stitch across the bottom of the hem.

6. Pin the right side of the pocket to the wrong side of the pillow front, lining up the pocket with the bottom edge of the pillow front; pin around the three outside edges. Stitch around the pocket edge. Clip the corners and turn the pillow front inside out. Press the pillow front with the newly added pocket.

7. Arrange the pillow front against the pillow back, right sides together. Pin around the sides and bottom of the fabric layers and stitch around the outside with a ½-inch (1.3 cm) seam allowance.

8. Turn the pillowcase inside out.

9. Stuff the pillow form inside the case.

10. Topstitch the pillow shut along the 2-inch (5.1 cm) hemline.

FAT QUARTER PARTY HATS

Create a custom celebration with fat quarters. Festive and fun, these hats also make nice mementos when the party is done.

DESIGN BY CYNTHIA SHAFFER

6 FAT Quarters

FINISHED SIZE
- 6½ inches (16.5 cm) tall

MATERIALS (TO MAKE ALL THREE)
- 6 fat quarters: 5 in coordinating blues, teals, and turquoise prints; 1 in a green-and-blue print
- Basic Sewing Kit (page 2)
- Templates (page 148)
- Lightweight fusible interfacing, ⅓ yard (30.5 cm)
- Fabric glue stick
- 35 inches (88.9 cm) of single-fold bias tape, black
- 1 black button, ¾ inch (1.9 cm) in diameter
- 3⅓ yards (3 m) of ribbon, ¼ inch (6 mm) wide
- 2 fabric scraps: 1 black, 1 white with black polka dots
- Fusible web, 7 inches square (17.8 cm)
- 7 black buttons, ½ inch (1.3 cm) in diameter

INSTRUCTIONS

Hat #1: Striped Yo-Yo Hat

1. Cut three 3 x 13-inch (7.6 x 33 cm) strips from three of the coordinating fat quarters.

2. Machine-stitch the strips together along the long edge, right sides together, using a ¼-inch (6 mm) seam allowance. Press all the seams in the same direction.

3. Place template A on top of the pieced panel from step 2. Center the template, trace around it, and cut out the shape. Transfer markings with a water-soluble marker.

4. Cut out template B from the lightweight fusible interfacing.

Transfer all marks onto the non-fusible side.

5. With right sides facing, pin the fabric hat shape along the straight sides and then stitch using a ¼-inch (6 mm) seam allowance. Turn the hat right side out and press the seam allowance open. Use a straight pin to poke the very tip of the hat out to a point.

6. Apply fabric glue to the hat cut from interfacing along one of the straight edges. Overlap this edge with the other straight edge and press into place. Make sure that the fusible surface is on the outside of the hat.

7. Insert the interfacing hat into the fabric hat, aligning the seam of the

fabric hat and the overlapped portion of the interfacing hat. Press the two hats together with the iron.

8. Pin the bias tape around the bottom edge of the hat and stitch in place.

9. Use template C and cut out a circle from the green fabric.

10. With a hand-sewing needle and thread, make a long running stitch (page 5) about ¼ inch (6 mm) from the outer edge of the circle. Draw up the stitching to make a gathered circle, or yo-yo. Secure the end of the thread with a knot.

11. Stitch the yo-yo to the outside of the hat, at the center front, on the

seam where the first two fabrics meet. Stitch the ¾-inch (1.9 cm) black button to the center of the yo-yo.

12. Cut two lengths of ribbon each measuring 19 inches (48.3 cm). Machine-stitch the ribbons to the inside of the hat at the marks.

Hat #2: Celebration Hat

1. Place template A on top of the blue fat quarter and cut out. Transfer all marks.

2. Use template B and cut out one piece from the lightweight fusible interfacing. Transfer all marks onto the non-fusible side.

3. With right sides facing, pin the fabric hat shape along the straight sides and then stitch using a ¼-inch (6 mm) seam allowance. Turn the hat right side out and press the seam allowance open. Use a straight pin to poke the very tip of the hat out to a point.

4. Apply fabric glue to the hat shape cut from interfacing along one of the straight edges. Overlap this edge with the other straight edge and press into place. Make sure that the fusible surface is on the outside of the hat.

5. Insert the interfacing hat into the fabric hat, aligning the seam of the fabric hat and the overlapped portion of the interfacing hat. Press the two hats together with the iron.

6. Pin the bias tape around the bottom edge of the hat and stitch in place.

7. Trace templates C, D, and E onto the paper side of the square of fusible web and cut out the shapes, close to but not on the traced line.

8. Following the manufacturer's instructions, fuse the web to the wrong side of the green, black, and white-and-black polka-dot fabrics. Cut out the shapes on the traced line, then peel off the paper backing.

9. Center the large circle on the hat and iron in place. Center the black circle on it and iron in place, and then iron the number 2 in place.

10. Cut two lengths of ribbon each measuring 19 inches (48.3 cm), Machine-stitch the ribbons to the inside of the hat at the marks.

Hat #3: Ruffled Hat

1. Follow steps 1 through 5 for Hat #2.

2. Cut a strip of green fabric that measures 1¼ x 30 inches (3.2 x 76.2 cm). Because the fat quarter is only 18 x 22 inches (45.7 x 55.9 cm), you will have to piece this strip together.

3. Machine-baste down the center of the strip.

4. Pull the top basting thread and gather it up until the strip measures 14 inches (35.6 cm).

5. Pin the gathered strip to the bottom edge of the hat and machine-stitch it in place.

6. Hand-sew seven ½-inch (1.3 cm) black buttons, evenly spaced around the hat, to the center of the gathered strip.

7. Cut two lengths of ribbon each measuring 19 inches (48.3 cm). Machine-stitch the ribbons to the inside of the hat at the marks.

FINISHED SIZE

- 15 x 12½ inches (38.1 x 31.8 cm)

MATERIALS

- 3 fat quarters: 2 of fabric A for the dress,
  1 of fabric B for contrasting border and bias trim
- Basic Sewing Kit (page 2)
- Templates (page 149)
- Coordinating thread
- Serger (optional)
- 1 yard (0.9 m) of rickrack trim

- **NOTE:** *Fabrics should all be quilting-weight cotton. Check the direction of the fabric's printing. If there is a direction, be sure the pattern is oriented to run the width of the fat quarter—so the 22-inch (55.9 cm) side is at the top—or buy ¾ yard (68.6 cm) in a traditional cut to be certain you have enough length either parallel or perpendicular to the selvedge.*

FQ BABY DRESS

It's got lovely rickrack trim and a chunky hem. So grab a couple of fat quarters and make this stylish dress for the special babe in your life.

DESIGN BY ANNELIESE

3
FAT
Quarters

INSTRUCTIONS

1. Fold each fabric A fat quarter in half widthwise.

2. Cut fabrics as follows:

- One dress Front on the fold, and two of the dress Back from fabric A.
- Two pieces off the short end of fabric B for the border, each measuring 17 x 5 inches (43.2 x 12.7 cm).

3. Use the remainder of fabric B to make ½-inch (1.3 cm) double-fold bias tape (see Make Your Own Binding on page 10). You should have a bit more than you need to make a strip of bias tape measuring 34 inches (86.4 cm) long.

4. Place the two dress Back pieces right sides together. Sew the center seam with a ¼-inch (6 mm) seam allowance, stitching from the hem to 3 inches (7.6 cm) below the neck. Baste from this point to the neck edge. Finish the seam allowance by zigzagging or serging.

5. Press the seam open and unpick the basting stitches.

6. Lay the dress Back on the dress Front, right sides together, and pin the shoulder and side seams. Stitch these seams using a ½-inch (1.3 cm) seam allowance. Trim the seam allowance to less than ¼ inch (6 mm) and zigzag-stitch or serge to finish.

7. Hem the sleeves of the dress by turning under the raw edges twice so they are as narrow as possible (between ⅛ and ¼ inches (3 and 6 mm). Stitch close to the folded edge (see Figure 1).

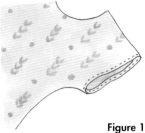

Figure 1

8. Apply rickrack to the bottom of the dress by pinning its center ½ inch (1.3 cm) from the raw edge of the dress. Overlap the ends and angle them down past the edge of the dress. Baste down the center of the rickrack using a ½-inch (1.3 cm) seam allowance.

9. Fold each 17 x 5-inch (43.2 x 12.7 cm) border piece in half lengthwise, wrong sides together, and press. Fold under the bottom edge of each piece ½ inch (1.3 cm) and press.

10. Stack the border pieces right sides together with the folded bottom edges and raw top edges aligned. Pin along the short edges. Check the width of these border pieces against the dress and adjust seam allowances on the border pieces to fit if necessary. Stitch the short edges.

11. With right sides together, pin the top of the contrasting border to the dress hem, matching the side seams. Stitch with a ½-inch (1.3 cm) seam allowance.

12. Press the seam allowances down toward the border.

13. Fold the border piece in half along the pressing line and pin the pressed, folded bottom to the wrong side of the dress at the border/dress seam.

14. On the right side of the dress, topstitch close to the border seam to finish.

15. Using a machine basting stitch and a ½-inch (1.3 cm) seam allowance, gather the neck edge of the dress.

16. At the neck, mark the center of the dress Front. Mark the center of the 34-inch (86.4 cm) piece of bias binding. Mark 10 inches (25.4 cm) on either side of the center.

With the bias binding unfolded, pin the right side of the binding to the wrong side of the dress along the neck edge as follows: pin the center of the binding to the center of the dress, and the two 10-inch marks at the back neck opening. On the binding, find both centers between the back pins and the front center pin and match those to the shoulder seams. Pull the gathers to evenly distribute them, and fit the neck opening between the pins (see Figure 2).

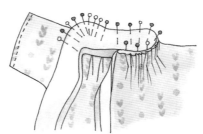

Figure 2

17. Stitch the binding to the neck edge using a ½-inch (1.3 cm) seam allowance. Trim the neck edge to ¼ inch (6 mm). Fold the bias binding over the neck along the pressing lines so it encases the neck gathers. Pin well along the neck edge, then pin all the way down to the ends, turning the raw ends under ½ inch (1.3 cm) before folding.

18. Stitch as close as possible to the folded edges of the bias tape to finish.

FINISHED SIZE

- Apple: 5 x 5 x 6 inches (12.7 x 12.7 x 15.2 cm)
- Worm: 1 x 6 inches (2.5 x 15.2 cm)

MATERIALS

- 3 fat quarters: 1 of fabric A (solid red), 1 of fabric B (red polka-dotted), and 1 of fabric C (green)
- Basic Sewing Kit (page 2)
- Templates (page 150)
- 1 piece of batting, 4 x 6 inches (10.2 x 15.2 cm)
- Scrap of light pink wool-blend felt
- Coordinating all-purpose thread
- 4 inches (10.2 cm) of brown cord
- Highlighter or other wide marker (to use as a placeholder)
- 5.3 ounces (150.3 g) of polyester fiberfill
- Stuffing tool such as a chopstick or hemostat
- Embroidery needle
- 12 inches (30.5 cm) of size 8 pink perle cotton
- 12 inches (30.5 cm) of size 8 black perle cotton
- Glue (optional)
- NOTES: *All seam allowances are ¼ inch (6 mm) unless otherwise indicated.*

  Cut along the templates' solid lines and stitch along the dotted lines. Topstitching on the leaf is marked with dotted and dashed lines.

TOY APPLE WITH WORM

Homemade toys are the best, especially when they're interactive. Wee hands will stay busy putting the worm in and out of his cozy apple home.

DESIGN BY ABBY GLASSENBERG

3 FAT Quarters

INSTRUCTIONS

1. Cut fabrics as follows:

- Two Apple pieces without holes from fabric A.
- Two Apple pieces from fabric B, one with a hole and one without.
- Two Pocket pieces from fabric B, one with a hole and one without.
- Two Leaf pieces from fabric C, reversing one.
- One Leaf piece from the batting.
- Two Worm pieces from fabric C, reversing one.
- Two Cheeks from the pink felt.

Transfer all markings to the fabric with a disappearing fabric marker or chalk.

2. Place the two Leaf pieces right sides together. Line up the batting Leaf underneath to create a three-layer sandwich: batting and two fabric layers. Stitch around the Leaf, leaving the opening at the base as marked. Clip the curves and trim

the seam allowance at the tip to reduce bulk. Turn the Leaf right side out and press. Topstitch the veins with coordinating green thread. Fold the leaf in half vertically and baste the base to hold. Set aside.

3. Fold the brown cord in half and tie a knot at the tip. Set aside.

4. Place the Pocket piece with the hole in it on top of the fabric B Apple piece that has the hole in it, right sides together. Use the notches on the holes to align them. Stitch in a circle, ¼ inch (6 mm) outside the hole. Go all the way around (see Figure 1). Clip the seam allowance inside the hole. Push the Pocket piece through the hole to the wrong side of the Apple piece. Smooth the fabric around the hole. Press flat with a steam iron.

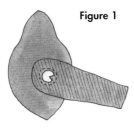

Figure 1

5. Place the second pocket piece on top of the first, right sides together. Pin. Then stitch around the pocket only (see Figure 2).

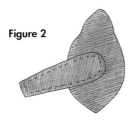

Figure 2

6. Place the polka-dotted Apple piece with the sewn pocket on top of a solid Apple piece, right sides together. Align and stitch from points A to B.

7. Place the leaf and the cord at point A on the portion of the apple assembled thus far. Align the raw edge of the leaf and the knot in the cord with the edge of the fabric where the two wedges meet. Baste in place.

8. Place the assembled polka-dotted piece from Step 6 with the remaining polka-dotted piece, right sides together. Align and stitch points A to B. Leave the opening as marked on the Apple pattern piece.

9. Both sides together, stitch the final solid red apple piece to the assembled pieces from point A to point B on each side. The raw edges of the leaf and the cord will be caught in the seams as you sew the apple wedges together. Remove the basting.

10. Place the assembled apple on your work surface, pocket side up. Pin the seam allowance at the tip of the pocket to the seam allowance of the apple where wedge 2 and wedge 3 meet. Stitch the seam allowances together to hold the pocket in place.

11. Clip all curves. Carefully turn the apple right side out through the opening.

12. Push a highlighter (or other cylindrical object) into the hole in the apple to prevent it from being crushed by stuffing. The marker serves as a placeholder for the worm.

13. Stuff the apple firmly. Pay careful attention to the humps at the top and bottom that give it a truly apple-like shape. Periodically wiggle the marker to be sure there is space for the worm to fit into the hole. Close the opening with a ladder stitch (page 5).

14. Place the two worm pieces right sides together and stitch around. Leave the opening as marked on the template. Clip the curves, turn the worm right side out, and press. Stuff the worm firmly and close the opening with a ladder stitch.

15. Thread an embroidery needle with a 12-inch (30.5 cm) length of pink perle cotton. Stitch the worm's mouth with a backstitch (page 5). Hide the knots where the cheeks will go.

16. Thread an embroidery needle with a 12-inch (30.5 cm) length of black perle cotton. Make two French knots (page 5), right next to each other, for the eyes. Hide the knots where the cheeks will go.

17. Glue or stitch the cheeks in place.

FLOPPY ANIMAL FRIENDS

They're soft, huggable, and a little floppy—these animals are perfect for little ones to snuggle!

DESIGN BY MOLLIE JOHANSON

2 FAT Quarters

FINISHED SIZE
- Body: 4¼ x 6 inches (10.8 x 15.2 cm)
- With arms, legs, and ears: 10 x 9 inches (25.4 x 22.9 cm)

MATERIALS (MAKES ONE ANIMAL)
- 2 coordinating fat quarters: 1 of fabric A, 1 of fabric B
- Basic Sewing Kit (page 2)
- Templates (page 151)
- Cotton batting, 6 x 8 inches (15.2 x 20.3 cm)
- White felt, 3 x 4 inches (7.6 x 10.2 cm)
- Featherweight fusible interfacing, 3 x 4 inches (7.6 x 10.2 cm)
- Felt to contrast with fabric, 3 x 4½ inches (7.6 x 11.4 cm)
- Embroidery floss in a color to complement fabrics, black, and pink
- Polyester fiberfill
- **NOTE:** *All seam allowances are ¼ inch (6 mm) unless otherwise indicated.*

INSTRUCTIONS

1. Cut fabric as follows:
- Two pieces from fabric A for the body, 5 x 7 inches (12.7 x 17.8 cm).
- Four each of Arms, Legs, and Ears (two regular and two reversed) from fabric B.
- Two each of Arms, Legs, and Ears from cotton batting.
- Face template A from white felt.
- Face template B from interfacing.
- Bow and Heart templates from contrasting felt.

2. Sew the Ears, Arms, and Legs together: for each, layer the batting and then the two fabric pieces, right sides together. Pin and sew around each shape, leaving the straight edge open for turning. Clip the curves and turn each shape right side out.

3. Use a running stitch (page 5) with three strands of complementary embroidery floss to stitch the Bow pieces in place on the front body piece, layering the center over the larger Bow shape. Stitch the Heart on the back body piece with the floss.

4. Baste the Ears, Arms, and Legs to the right side of one body piece with the Ears and limbs facing in; the straight edges should align with the sides of the body piece. If the Bow is near the edge, fold the sides in and hand-baste them down so they won't get caught in the seams.

5. With right sides together, sew the body pieces together, leaving a 2-inch (5.1 cm) opening for turning. Clip the corners and turn your animal right side out. Fill the body with fiberfill, but do not overstuff. Stitch the opening closed with a ladder stitch (page 5).

6. Embroider the Face on the felt face piece with three strands of embroidery floss. Use a satin stitch (page 5) for the eyes and nose, and use a backstitch (page 5) for the mouth and to outline the eyes.

7. Use a running stitch with three strands of pink embroidery floss to stitch the Face piece and interfacing to the front of the animal, stitching through to the back so that the face has a bit of puffiness. Stitch around the outside edge of the animal with a running stitch.

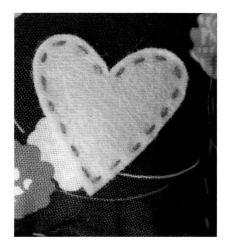

✕ ✕ ✕ ✕ ✕ ✕ ✕ ✕ ✕

TIP: Instead of making your animal with contrasting ears, arms, and legs, use one fat quarter for the entire animal. Add a sensory element for little ones by sewing crinkle paper into the arms and legs!

✕ ✕ ✕ ✕ ✕ ✕ ✕ ✕ ✕

FINISHED SIZE

• 18-inch circle when open

MATERIALS

• 2 fat quarters: 1 of fabric A (low-contrast print), 1 of fabric B, plus scraps
• Basic Sewing Kit (page 2)
• Templates (page 152)
• 3 pieces of fabric, each 4 x 12 inches (10.2 x 30.5 cm): 1 of fabric C; 1 of fabric D; 1 of fabric E (different colored prints or solids, can be cut from fat quarters)
• Paper-backed fusible interfacing, 4 x 8 inches (10.2 x 20.3 cm)
• 9-inch (22.9 cm) piece of string
• Embroidery floss in white and black
• 3½ yards (3.2 m) of twill tape, ½ inch (1.3 cm) wide
• Polyester fiberfill
• NOTE: *All seam allowances are ¼ inch (6mm) unless otherwise indicated.*

SOFT-SHAPED TOYS & POUCH

Help baby learn his shapes with this sweet (and soft!) playmat toy. Simply spread the mat and match the shapes, then pull the drawstring to pack up and go.

DESIGN BY MOLLIE JOHANSON

2 FAT Quarters

INSTRUCTIONS

1. Cut fabric as follows:

• Two 18-inch (45.7 cm) circles for the play mat, one from each fat quarter. (See the tip.)

• Three triangle template shapes from fabric C (cut on template solid lines).

• Three circle template shapes from fabric D (cut on template solid lines).

• Three square template shapes from fabric E (cut on template solid lines).

• One smaller piece of each shape (cut on template dotted lines) from the interfacing.

2. Iron the fusible interfacing shapes to the back of one of its corresponding

✕ ✕ ✕ ✕ ✕ ✕ ✕ ✕ ✕

✕   **TIP: To cut the 18-inch**   ✕
✕   **(45.7 cm) circles, fold**   ✕
✕   **the fabric into quarters.**
✕   **Tie a 9-inch (22.9 cm)**   ✕
✕   **string to a pencil, then,**
✕   **holding the end of the**   ✕
✕   **string at the folded**
✕   **fabric corner, mark out**   ✕
✕   **the quarter circle arc**
✕   **and cut along the line.**   ✕

✕ ✕ ✕ ✕ ✕ ✕ ✕ ✕ ✕

shapes of fabric, making sure they are centered. Before removing the paper backing, fold and press the edges of

the square and triangle toward the paper. For the circle, hand-stitch along the edge with a loose running stitch (page 5), then gather in the edges and press with an iron.

3. Remove the paper backing and iron the shapes to the center of the fabric A circle. Stitch around the edge of each shape with a running stitch, using three strands of white embroidery floss.

4. Cut eight 3-inch (7.6 cm) strips of twill tape. Fold each one in half and pin evenly around the fabric A circle with the fold facing in and the raw edges aligned with the edge of the circle. Baste the tabs in place.

5. Lay the fabric B circle over A, with right sides together. Pin and sew around the circle, leaving a 2- to 3-inch (5.1 to 7.6 cm) opening. Clip the curves, turn the circle right side out, and close the opening with a ladder stitch (page 5).

6. Stitch around the play-mat circle with a running stitch, using three strands of white embroidery floss. Thread the remaining twill tape through the tabs to gather the play mat into a bag. Knot the ends together. When gathered, tie the drawstring into a bow.

CAUTION: When the play mat is flat, the drawstring should lie flat with no extra loop of twill tape. Never let a baby play with the bag when the bag is gathered and the drawstring is loose.

7. Use the remaining two pieces of fabrics C, D, and E to make the soft-shape toys: Embroider a face onto one of each shape with black floss.

✕ ✕ ✕ ✕ ✕ ✕ ✕ ✕ ✕

✕ **TIP: Position the** ✕
✕ **stitched face so that it** ✕
✕ **doesn't get lost in the** ✕
✕ **design of the fabric.** ✕

✕ ✕ ✕ ✕ ✕ ✕ ✕ ✕ ✕

8. Pin the matching shaped pieces right sides together and sew around the edges, leaving a small opening for turning. Clip the curves and corners. Turn the shapes right side out.

9. Fill the shapes with fiberfill and close the openings with a ladder stitch.

DIAPER HOLDER & BURP CLOTH

Yes, this is the perfect last-minute baby shower gift. Even better? It makes diaper changes that much more stylish and easy.

DESIGN BY BEKI LAMBERT

2 FAT Quarters

FINISHED SIZE
- Pouch: 6 ⅛ x 9½ inches (15.6 x 24.1 cm) plus 3-inch (7.6 cm) flap
- Burp cloth: 10¾ x 20½ inches (27.3 x 52.1 cm)

MATERIALS
- 2 coordinating fat quarters
- Basic Sewing Kit (page 2)
- Template (page 152)
- Matching thread
- Hook-and-loop tape
- 1 piece of flannel, 11 x 22 inches (27.9 x 55.9 cm)*

- **NOTES:** *An old receiving blanket is a perfect choice.*

  All seam allowances are ¼ inch (6 mm) unless otherwise indicated.

INSTRUCTIONS

1. Cut one fat quarter so that it is divided into two pieces: one 11 x 22 inches (27.9 x 55.9 cm) and the other 7 x 22 inches (17.8 x 55.9 cm). Repeat for the second fat quarter. The wider pieces will be used for the burp cloth, while the others will be used for the diaper wipes pouch.

2. To create the curved flap on the pouch, use the template to cut one short side of the pouch pieces. Keep the direction of your fabric in mind when choosing which end to cut.

3. Position both pouch pieces right sides together. Beginning on a short end (opposite the curved end), sew around the entire pouch, leaving a 4-inch (10.2 cm) opening on the short end where you began.

4. Clip the two squared corners and trim the fabric seam allowance along the curve.

5. Using the 4-inch (10.2 cm) opening, turn the pouch right side out.

6. Smooth out the fabric then press with an iron.

7. Turn in the raw edges and sew along the short end of the pouch close to the edge, closing up the opening.

8. On the lining side of the pouch at the curved edge, position one piece of the hook-and-loop tape at the center of the pouch with the center of the tape about ½ inch (1.3 cm) from the curved edge. Sew in place. On the exterior side of the pouch at the short edge, position the other piece of the hook-and-loop tape at the center of the pouch about ½ inch (1.3 cm) from the edge. Sew in place.

9. With the lining fabric facing you, fold the short end of the pouch up toward the curved edge 8 inches (20.3 cm). Pin in place.

10. Beginning at a bottom corner, sew up one side, around the curve of the flap, then down the other side. Be sure to backstitch at the beginning and end of this seam.

11. To create the burp cloth, place the two 11 x 22-inch (27.9 x 55.9 cm) pieces right sides together. Layer the piece of flannel on top of the two fat-quarter pieces. Pin the layers together.

12. Stitch the layers together by sewing around the pieces, leaving a 4-inch (10.2 cm) opening where you began.

13. Use the opening to turn the fabric right side out. You should end up with the two fat quarter pieces facing out with the flannel layered between them. Smooth the fabric then press with an iron.

14. Turn in the opening's raw edges and topstitch along all four sides of the burp cloth, closing up the opening in the process.

FINISHED SIZE

- 8½ inches square (21.6 cm)

MATERIALS

- 2 fat quarters: 1 of fabric A (main body of the purse), 1 of fabric B (lining and mushroom cap)
- Basic Sewing Kit (page 2)
- Fusible adhesive
- Templates (page 153)
- Assorted fabric scraps for mushroom dots, door, window, and curtains
- 1 batting remnant, 8 x 6 inches (20.3 x 15.2 cm)
- Coordinating threads and embroidery floss
- 1 magnetic snap closure, ¾ inch (1.9 cm)
- 1 small button (for door handle)
- 2 small flower trims
- 1 yard (0.9 m) of webbing, 1 inch (2.5 cm) wide

MUSHROOM TOTE

Perfect for stowing notes, a journal and pen, or a stash of precious treasures from a nature walk, this purse is just the thing for the on-the-go little lady in your life.

DESIGNED BY HEATHER VALENTINE

2 FAT Quarters

INSTRUCTIONS

1. Cut fabric as follows:

- One piece from fabric A, 20½ x 9¼ inches (52.1 x 23.5 cm).
- One piece from fabric B, 17½ x 9¼ inches (44.5 x 23.5 cm).
- Two Mushroom Caps from fabric B.
- One piece of fusible adhesive, 19 ¾ x 8¼ inches (50.2 x 21 cm).

2. Trace the Door, Window, Curtains, and Mushroom Dots templates on the paper side of the fusible adhesive. Follow manufacturer's instructions and apply to the wrong side of fabric scraps as desired. Cut out the appliqué shapes.

3. Using the pieces cut from step 1, center and fuse the fusible adhesive to the wrong side of main fabric A.

NOTE: The lining is used to clean finish the appliqué stitching and can be omitted from the project. It does not clean finish all seams.

4. Position and fuse the Mushroom Dots in place on the right side of one Mushroom Cap. Layer the Mushroom Cap on top of batting remnant. With coordinating thread, machine-sew all around the edge of Mushroom Dots through all layers using a small zigzag or satin stitch.

5. Sandwich both Mushroom Cap pieces right sides together and straight stitch all around with a ⅜-inch (9.5 mm) seam allowance, leaving a 2-inch (5.1 cm) opening at the top for turning. Clip the seam allowance around all curves. Turn the Mushroom Cap right side out and press.

NOTE: If necessary, use a dull object to smooth curves from the inside.

6. Turn under the ⅜-inch (9.5 mm) seam allowance along the opening, press, and stitch closed. Set aside.

7. To make the main bag, fold and press ½-inch (1.3 cm) seam allowance over the fusible adhesive on each short side of fabric from step 3; this is your clean-finished hem edge. Fold

over 1¼ inches (3.2 cm), press, and find the center. Attach magnetic snap closure following the manufacturer's instructions.

NOTE: It is important that the snap be placed toward the top edge of hem.

8. Position and fuse the appliqué pieces in place. For the Door, Window, and Curtains, stitch all around with a coordinating thread or floss color and decorative blanket stitch (page 5). With a contrasting color, add two lines of stitching to create panes in the window. Add the button for the doorknob and flower trims.

9. Layer the lining (fabric B) over the fusible adhesive and tuck under the fold of hem, pin in place, and stitch across the hemline (see Figure 1). Repeat to other side.

Figure 1

10. Position the Mushroom Cap on the bag and stitch through all layers using ¼-inch (6 mm) seam allowance (see Figure 2).

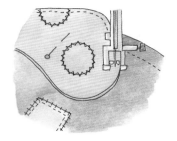

Figure 2

11. Fold the bag right sides together, matching the hemmed edge and straight-stitch the side seams. Consider adding a zigzag or overlock edge to finish the seam.

12. Create boxed corners (page 6) by pinching each corner together and then stitching a perpendicular line ¾ inch (1.9 cm) from the point of each corner. Trim and repeat on the opposite corner. Consider adding an additional row of stitching for reinforcement.

13. Decide how long you'd like the straps to be (based on your child's height), add 2 inches (5.1 cm) for overlap, and cut the webbing to this measurement. Center the webbing over the side seam; pin in place 1 inch (2.5 cm) below top edge and straight-stitch in position. Fold the webbing up toward the hem (back on itself) and box-stitch in place. Repeat on the other side.

14. Trim all loose threads and press purse as needed.

BABY FOOD JAR BIB

Mushy peas, carrots, or applesauce, recreate baby's favorite foods with this sweet paper-pieced bib.

DESIGN BY JENNIFER RODRIGUEZ

3 FAT Quarters

FINISHED SIZE
- 8½ x 12 inches (21.6 x 30.5 cm)

MATERIALS
- 3 fat quarters: 1 of fabric A for bib backing, 1 of fabric B for bib front, 1 of fabric C for the baby jar and binding
- Basic Sewing Kit (page 2)
- Template (page 153)
- Fusible fleece, 18 x 21 inches (45.7 x 53.3 cm)
- 4-inch (10.2 cm) square of fabric for jar lid
- 1 sheet of copy paper
- Glue stick
- Matching thread
- Snap
- **NOTE:** *All seam allowances are ¼ inch (6 mm) unless otherwise indicated.*

INSTRUCTIONS

1. Trace the bib template onto the fusible fleece and fabric A, then cut both out.

2. Trace the paper-piecing template onto the copy paper. Using the paper piecing template sections as a guide, cut rough shapes (larger than necessary) from fabric B for the background pieces, fabric C for the baby jar piece, and the scrap for the lid piece. Foundation paper piece to create the bib front (pages 6–7).

3. Following the manufacturer's instructions, iron the fusible fleece down to the wrong side of the bib front.

4. Pin the bib front to the fabric A bib back with wrong sides together. With a ⅛-inch (3 mm) seam allowance, baste them together.

5. Cut fabric C into 2-inch (5.1 cm) strips on the bias and piece together to create the binding (page 10). Machine-sew the binding onto the bib front and hand-sew onto the back.

6. Thread a hand-sewing needle and sew the snap onto the bib collar ends.

CHILD'S TRAVEL PLACEMAT

Contain snack-time messes with this portable placemat. The vinyl wipes off easily, and the handy strap means you can roll it up and go.

DESIGN BY JENNIFER RODRIGUEZ

3 FAT Quarters

FINISHED SIZE
- 15 x 11½ inches (38.1 x 29.2 cm)

MATERIALS
- 3 fat quarters of different colors: 1 each of fabric A, fabric B, and fabric C (I used blue, orange, and brown, respectively)
- Basic Sewing Kit (page 2)
- 16 x 12 inches (40.6 x 30.5 cm) of fusible vinyl
- Cotton-blend batting
- Templates (page 154)
- 1 scrap of fabric D for the stems (I used green)
- Fusible web
- Thread
- Sew-on hook-and-loop tape, 1 inch square (2.5 cm)
- **NOTE:** *All seam allowances are ¼ inch (6 mm) unless otherwise indicated.*

INSTRUCTIONS

1. Cut materials as follows:

- One piece from fabric A for the placemat top, 6½ x 17 inches (16.5 x 43.2 cm).
- Two pieces from fabric A for the straps, each 4 x 20 inches (10.2 x 50.8 cm).
- One piece from fabric B for the placemat back, 12¼ x 17 inches (31.1 x 43.2 cm).
- One piece from fabric C for the placemat top, 6½ x 17 inches (16.5 x 43.2 cm).
- Three pieces from fabric C for the binding strips, each 2 x 21 inches (5.1 x 53.3 cm).

- Two pieces from fusible vinyl, each 12¼ x 17 inches (31.1 x 43.2 cm).
- One piece from cotton-blend batting, 12¼ x 17 inches (31.1 x 43.2 cm).

2. With right sides together, sew the larger fabric A and fabric C pieces together along one of the long sides. This is your placemat top.

3. Using the templates, copy the carrots and stems onto fabric B and D scraps. Following the manufacturer's directions, iron the fusible web onto the back of those fabrics. Cut the shapes out and iron them onto the placemat top, using the photo as a guide.

4. Create a quilt sandwich: top, batting, and backing. Free-motion quilt the sandwich in your desired style (page 8). Square up the quilt sandwich if needed.

5. Following manufacturer's directions, iron the two cut pieces of fusible vinyl onto the front and back of the placemat.

6. With right sides of the fabric A strap pieces together, sew both long edges and one short edge. Clip the corners off and turn it right side out.

7. Sew the three fabric C binding strips together, then fold the strip lengthwise and iron.

8. Pin the strap to the placemat front. Machine-sew the binding to the placemat front (see pages 9–10).

9. Machine- or hand-sew the binding to the placemat back.

10. Machine-sew the hook-and-loop square onto the strap so that the pieces meet up when the strap is wrapped around the mat.

BAGS

FINISHED SIZE

- 7 x 7 x 3 inches (17.8 x 17.8 x 7.6 cm)

MATERIALS

- 2 fat quarters: 1 of fabric A for exterior, 1 of fabric B for interior lining
- Basic Sewing Kit (page 2)
- Scraps of red prints for red cross (fabric C)
- Rotary cutter and mat
- Fusible fleece, 18 x 21 inches (45.7 x 53.3 cm)
- Coordinating thread
- Scrap for interior pockets (fabric D), 7 x 15 inches (17.8 x 38.1 cm)
- Red plastic zipper, 24 inches (61 cm)
- **NOTE:** *All seam allowances are ¼ inch (6 mm) unless otherwise indicated.*

FIRST AID KIT

Complete with a pieced red cross pocket for storing essentials, this is a handy kit you can toss in your hiking bag. Why not stitch a few as gifts for your outdoorsy friends?

DESIGN BY AMY FRIEND

2 FAT Quarters

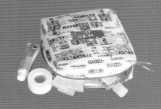

INSTRUCTIONS

1. Cut fabric into the following pieces:

- One from fabric A, 7½ inches square (19 cm).
- Two from fabric A, each 1½ x 2½ inches (3.8 x 6.4 cm).
- Four from fabric A, each 1½ x 3½ inches (3.8 x 8.9 cm).
- Two from fabric A, each 2½ x 7½ inches (6.4 x 19 cm).
- Two from fabric A, each 1½ x 20 inches (3.8 x 50.8 cm).
- One from fabric A, 3 x 9 inches (7.6 x 22.9 cm).
- Two from fabric B, each 7½ inches square (19 cm).

- Two from fabric B, each 1½ x 20 inches (3.8 x 50.8 cm).
- One from fabric B, 3 x 9 inches (7.6 x 22.9 cm).
- Four from fabric C, each 1½ inches square (3.8 cm).
- Two from fusible fleece, each 7½ inches square (19.1 cm).
- Two from fusible fleece, each 1½ x 20 inches (3.8 x 50.8 cm).
- One from fusible fleece, 3 x 9 inches (7.6 x 22.9 cm).
- Two scraps for zipper tabs, 2½ x 1½ inches (6.4 x 3.8 cm).

2. Piece the front of the bag. First sew a 1½ x 2½-inch (3.8 x 6.4 cm) strip of fabric A followed by three 1½-inch

(3.8 cm) squares of fabric C, followed by another 1½ x 2½-inch (3.8 x 6.4 cm) strip of fabric A. Then assemble the row above and below by joining two 1½ x 3½-inch (3.8 x 8.9 cm) strips of fabric A with a 1½-inch (3.8 cm) square of fabric C in the center. Join the five rows that make up the front: 2½ x 7½-inch (6.4 x 19 cm) strip of fabric A followed by the three pieced rows and one more 2½ x 7½-inch (6.4 x 19 cm) strip of fabric A (see Figure 1 on page 47).

3. Fuse fleece to the back of the pieced front and the back exterior piece (the 7½-inch [19 cm] square of fabric A).

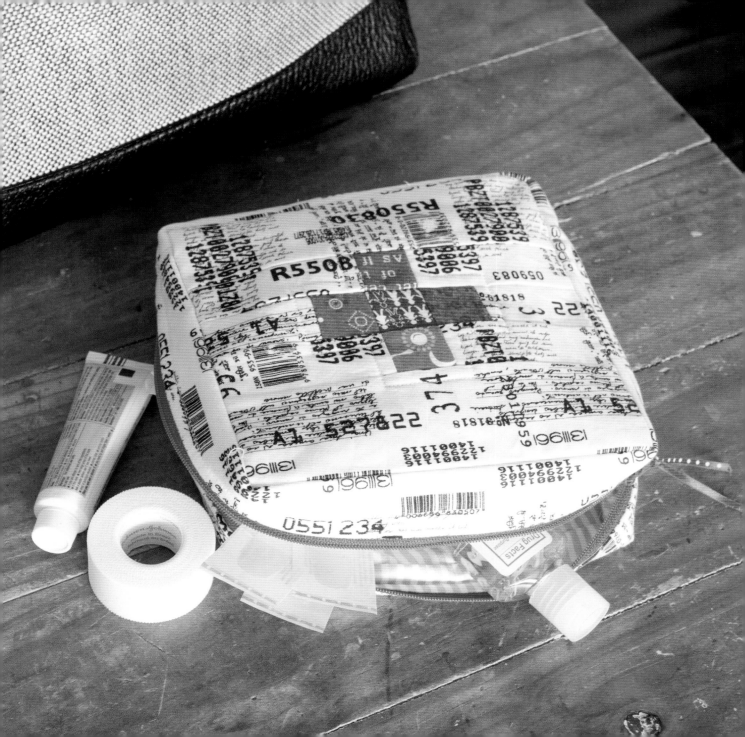

Figure 1

4. Fold a 7 x 15-inch (17.8 x 38.1 cm) strip of fabric D in half (wrong sides together) for the interior pocket, making 3½ x 15-inch (8.9 x 38.1 cm) strip. Make two rows of topstitching along the upper edge. Cut the piece into two 7½-inch (19 cm) lengths and align them with the lower edges of the two 7½-inch (19 cm) lining squares. Baste around the outer edges and then stitch some vertical lines for pockets (see Figure 2).

5. Fold under ¼ inch (6 mm) on both edges of the zipper tab pieces and then fold each in half to make a 1-inch (2.5 cm) tab. Cut the zipper at its metal tab and cover with one zipper tab. Stitch across. Measure the zipper and cut at about 19½ inches (49.5 cm) and cover with the other zipper tab so the full length of the zipper with tabs will be 20 inches (50.8 cm).

6. Take the two 2½ x 7½-inch (6.4 x 19 cm) strips of exterior fabric A that remain and fuse fleece to the back. Place one of these strips with right side down over the zipper unit. Place a long strip of lining fabric B right side up

below the zipper and stitch through all layers along the length of the zipper. With the lining fabric B on the underside and the exterior fabric A on top, press. Repeat for other side of the zipper. Do not topstitch along the edge of the zipper as you normally would.

7. Fuse the fleece to the 3 x 9-inch (7.6 x 22.9 cm) piece of fabric A. Sew each short end of this piece to the ends of the zipper, right sides together, to turn the zipper unit into a loop (see Figure 2). Do not stitch through zipper or lining: just stitch from the edge to the zipper and stop; restart on the other side of the zipper. Do the same with the lining. Then topstitch all the way around the zipper; in doing this, you will secure the area you did not stitch through near the zipper but still leave the outer edges of the lining and exterior fabric free all the way around.

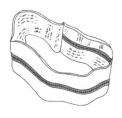

Figure 2

8. Orient the loop so that the zipper is going over the top of the bag and the zipperless part of the loop is on the bottom. Measure ¾ inch (1.9 cm) from the seam where the zipper unit is attached to the 3 x 9-inch

(7.6 x 22.9 cm) piece and place a pin. Do this on the other side as well. Then measure 7 inches (17.8 cm) from those two pins to mark the other corners of the bag.

9. Begin by orienting your bag front properly and then stitch it to the zipper loop unit, right sides together, stopping at each pin and pivoting all the way around the bag (see Figure 3). Make sure that the lining is out of the way while you do this so it doesn't get caught in your stitching.

Figure 3

10. Follow these same steps to attach the back exterior of the bag to the zipper loop unit (bag sides). Keep the zipper open while you do this.

11. Turn the bag right side out to make sure that it is as it should be and any directional prints in the red cross are heading in the right direction.

12. Next sew the lining fabric B pieces in the same manner. When attaching the final lining piece, leave an opening about 4 inches (10.2 cm) wide at the top. Turn the bag through that opening and hand-stitch the opening closed.

FINISHED SIZE

- 11¾ x 7¾ inches (30 x 19.7 cm)

MATERIALS

- 4 fat quarters: 1 of fabric A for outer main, 1 of fabric B for faux flap, 1 of fabric C for lining and loop, 1 of fabric D for tab
- Basic Sewing Kit (page 2)
- Template (page 155)
- Rotary cutter and mat (optional)
- Interfacing, medium to heavy weight
- Batting
- Coordinating thread
- 1 button, about 1 inch (2.5 cm) in diameter
- Washable (removable) fabric marker or tailor's chalk

- NOTE: *This tablet case was designed to fit the average-size tablet. In order to calculate the dimensions for a specific tablet, measure the size as accurately as possible or refer to the tablet manufacturer's specifications on their website. Add 3 inches (7.6 cm) to the tablet height (which actually becomes your tablet case's width because the tablet slides in sideways) and 2 inches (5.1 cm) to the width (this becomes your tablet case's height) to accommodate for the depth of the tablet and for the batting and interfacing you will be using.*

COOL TABLET CASE

Tote your tablet with stow-and-go style…and show off a few of your favorite fat quarters while you're at it. Made for a standard tablet size, this case is easily customized.

DESIGN BY SHANNON COOK

INSTRUCTIONS

1. Cut the fabrics as follows:

- Two pieces from fabric A, 13 x 9 inches (33 x 22.9 cm) each.
- Two pieces from fabric B, 13 x 4¼ inches (33 x 10.8 cm) each.
- Two pieces from fabric C, 13 x 9 inches (33 x 22.9 cm) each.
- One piece from fabric C, 4¾ x 2 inches (12 x 5.1 cm).
- Two pieces from fabric D, 2¼ x 6½ inches (5.7 x 16.5 cm) each.
- Two pieces from interfacing, 13 x 9 inches (33 x 22.9 cm) each.
- Two pieces from batting, 13 x 9 inches (33 x 22.9 cm) each.
- Two pieces from batting, 2¼ x 6½ inches (5.7 x 16.5 c m) each.

2. Place fabric B right side up and lay your Faux Flap template pattern piece on top, tracing the template with your washable fabric marker. Cut your pattern piece out. Repeat for your other fabric B. You will now have faux flaps for your case. With the fabric B pieces wrong side up, evenly press a ¼-inch (6 mm) fold around the bottom curved edge only. Go slowly and press precisely.

3. Place one fabric A piece right side up and lay one fabric B piece right side up on top of it, matching both long straight upper edges. Pin along the curve of the B portion, making sure the ¼-inch (6 mm) fold is lying nice and flat. Topstitch along the curved edge carefully. Press flat. Repeat steps 2 and 3 with the other B and A pieces.

4. You now have a front and back for your case. Iron the interfacing pieces onto the wrong sides of your front and back pieces.

5. To make the tab, lay the batting and fabric D pieces together in this order: batting, fabric right side up, fabric right side down, batting. The right sides of the two fabric pieces should be facing each other, with a piece of batting on the bottom and top of them.

6. Sew along three sides of the tab—the two long edges and only one short end—using a ¼-inch (6 mm) seam allowance. Leave one short end unsewn. Clip the corners, taking care not to cut through the sewing. Turn the tab right side out and press. Topstitch along the perimeter of your tab except for the unsewn short end. Press again.

7. To make the loop, press the 4¾ x 2-inch (12 x 5.1 cm) fabric C piece in half lengthwise, wrong sides together, matching both long sides.

8. Starting at the fold on one short end, sew the loop with a ¼-inch (6 mm) seam allowance, ending in the middle of the raw long edge. Leave a 1-inch (2.5 cm) unsewn opening, and continue sewing until you reach the folded edge of the other short end. Trim the corners, being careful not to clip through the stitching (see Figure 1).

Figure 1

9. Turn the loop right side out. Press flat and topstitch around the entire perimeter of the loop, taking care to close the opening you pulled the loop through. Work slowly and steadily and you'll be fine!

10. With the right side facing up, find and mark the center of the case front using a removable fabric marker. Measure 1½ inches (3.8 cm) up from the bottom of the faux flap and mark this with the fabric marker. Now find the center of the loop and mark this as well. Next match the center of the loop with the center of the case where you marked the 1½-inch (3.8 cm) measurement; pin the loop at both ends.

11. Starting on the left side of the loop, sew a 1-inch (2.5 cm) square to secure it to the case. Now stitch an X through it. Repeat for the right side of the loop.

12. Place the outer case pieces with right sides facing each other. Pin along the bottom and sides, leaving the long top edge unpinned. Sew along the sides and bottom with a ½-inch (1.3 cm) seam allowance. Clip the corners, being careful not to clip through your sewing. Turn right side out and press.

NOTE: If you would like a label on your case, this would be a great time to add it.

13. Next mark the center of the back outer case (the one without the loop sewn on) with a fabric marker. Now find and mark the center of the unsewn end of the tab. With the right side of the back outer case facing up and the tab's right side facing down, match the center of the unsewn end of the tab and the center of the case's top edge and pin in place. Baste along the top edge of the tab with a ¼-inch (6 mm) seam allowance.

14. Place the 13 x 9-inch (33 x 22.9 cm) fabric C lining pieces with right sides facing each other and then place a piece of batting on the bottom and one on the top. They will be in the following order: batting; lining, right side up; lining, right side down; batting. Pin along the sides and bottom of the lining, leaving the top edge unpinned.

15. Stitch along the sides and bottom edge with a ½-inch (1.3 cm) seam allowance. Clip the corners, taking care to not cut through your sewing, and trim the batting accordingly.

16. With the outer case right side out and the lining turned inside out, place the outer case inside the lining (see Figure 2). When looking inside your case, you will see the wrong side of the lining and the wrong side of your outer case.

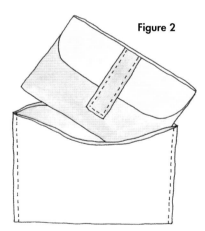

Figure 2

17. Check that your case is lined up and your side seams match up nicely. Pin the matched side seams, then continue to pin around the entire perimeter of the case. Sew along the top edge with a ½-inch (1.3 cm) seam allowance, making sure to leave a 4-inch (10.2 cm) opening to pull the case through. Trim the seam allowance.

18. Turn the case right side out. Before you push your lining inside, press if needed. Put the lining inside the case and press the outer case. Now is a good time to double-check and make sure your tablet fits in the case; make adjustments if needed.

19. Topstitch along the entire top perimeter of your case, taking care to close up the opening you pulled your case through. Press again.

20. Mark ¾ inch (1.9 cm) up from the bottom of the tab. This will be where your horizontal buttonhole will be. Following your sewing machine's instructions, make a buttonhole to match the button size you are using.

21. Pull the tab through the loop and mark with the fabric marker exactly where the button should be sewn to match up with the buttonhole. Hand-sew the button on your case, being careful to sew through your outer fabric only—not your lining as well.

FINISHED SIZE

• 15½ x 15 inches (39.4 x 38.1 cm)

MATERIALS

• 2 coordinating fat quarters for outside of bag
• Basic Sewing Kit (page 2)
• ¾ yard (68.6 cm) of fabric for lining and pocket
• 1¼ yard (114.3 cm) of lightweight interfacing
• Matching thread
• 1 sew-on snap, size 4 or larger
• 2 pieces of felt, each 2 inches square (5.1 cm)
• 1 strap, 84 inches (2.1 m) long and no wider than 1 inch (2.5 cm) (possible materials include rope, leather, canvas strapping)
• Heavy-duty sewing-machine needle (optional)
• NOTE: All seam allowances are ¼ inch (6 mm) unless otherwise indicated.

BOHO BAG

Oh, boho! This slouchy bag is pure and simple genius, great for stylish toting and for showcasing two special fat quarters.

DESIGN BY JESSICA FEDIW

2 FAT Quarters

INSTRUCTIONS

1. Cut fabric as follows:

• Halve both fat quarters along the 22-inch (55.9 cm) width, for two 9 x 22-inch (22.9 x 55.9 cm) pieces.

• One piece from the lining fabric, 22 x 34 inches (55.9 x 86.4 cm).

• Two additional pieces from the lining fabric for the pocket, each 7 x 9 inches (17.8 x 22.9 cm).

• One piece from the interfacing for the pocket, 7 x 9 inches (17.8 x 22.9 cm).

• One piece from the interfacing, 33 x 22 inches (83.9 x 55.9 cm).

2. Pin together one half of each fat quarter, matching up the widths and making sure the pattern on the fabric goes the same way, if applicable. Sew together. Repeat for the other two pieces.

3. Place the two outer pieces together, right sides facing and fabrics matching. Pin together and sew across the bottom width.

4. Use this piece as a pattern to trim the edges of the lining fabric so the measurements are the same. Cut the interfacing to the same size as well.

5. Now it's time to create the pocket. Place the 7 x 9-inch (17.8 x 22.9 cm) pocket pieces together, right sides facing, matching the edges. Place the interfacing piece on top. Pin together and sew around, leaving a 2-inch (5.1 cm) opening on the bottom for turning.

6. Turn the pocket right side out and push in the raw edges at the opening. Iron and then sew the opening shut.

7. Place the lining, right side facing up, on top of the interfacing. Center the pocket on top of lining fabric and 4 inches (10.2 cm) down on the left-hand short end. Make sure the top of the pocket is facing toward the left edge. Pin in place and then sew around three sides of the pocket, leaving the top edge open.

8. Sew each piece of the sew-on snap to a felt piece. Center one of these on the lining so that the bottom is 2½ inches (6.4 cm) above the pocket.

Sew in place as close to the snap as possible. Trim away the excess felt. Attach the other side of the snap.

9. Place the outer fabric on top of the lining piece, right sides facing. Match the edges and pin together.

10. Sew around the edge, leaving a 5-inch (12.7 cm) opening on one of the longer sides for turning.

11. Turn the bag right side out.

12. Turn in the raw edges at the opening and press. Sew it closed.

13. Topstitch around the whole piece ½ inch (1.3 cm) from edge.

14. Turn the edges in 3 inches (7.6 cm) on the long edges, lining sides facing, to make a casing. Pin in place.

15. Sew down the inner edges.

16. Thread the strap of choice through both side casings. Go through one side and then pull it through the other side. Connect the strap by sewing or knotting it together. Push that join into the casing so it will not be seen and adjust the strap so it is even on each end (see Figure 1).

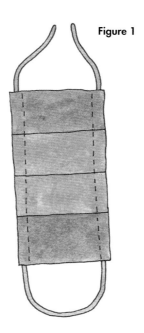

Figure 1

17. Fold the bag in half crosswise so the right side is facing out. Pin together.

18. Switch to the heavy-duty sewing machine needle, if needed. Sew the purse together by sewing just outside the fabric casing so you won't have to sew through as many layers (see Figure 2).

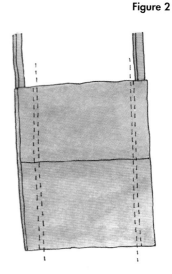

Figure 2

19. Pull the sides of the bag down to gather it some and make sure the strap lengths are still equal on both sides. When happy with how it looks, sew each of the openings of the four fabric casings to the purse strap to keep it in place.

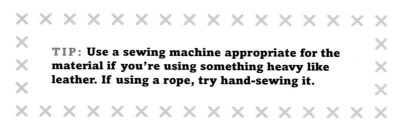

TIP: Use a sewing machine appropriate for the material if you're using something heavy like leather. If using a rope, try hand-sewing it.

LIBRARY TOTE

Tote a whole stack of your favorite tales with this sweet embroidered bag.

DESIGN BY TARA KOLESNIKOWICZ

EMBROIDERY DESIGN BY MOLLIE JOHANSON

3 FAT Quarters

FINISHED SIZE

- 14¼ x 18½ inches (36.2 x 47 cm)

MATERIALS

- 3 fat quarters: 1 of fabric A, 1 of fabric B, 1 of solid-colored fabric C
- Basic Sewing Kit (page 2)
- Interfacing
- Coordinating thread
- Book Motif template (page 155)
- Embroidery floss in several colors

INSTRUCTIONS

1. Cut fabric as follows:

- Two pieces from fabric A for straps, each 3 x 18 (7.6 x 45.7 cm).
- Two pieces from fabric B, each 16½ x 15½ inches (41.9 x 39.4 cm).
- Two pieces from fabric C, each 6½ x 15 inches (16.5 x 38.1 cm).
- Two pieces from interfacing, each 1 x 18 inches (2.5 x 45.7 cm).

2. To make the straps, fold the pieces of fabric A in half lengthwise with wrong sides together and press.

3. Place the interfacing inside along the fold. Fold one outside edge in over the interfacing and fold in the other edge to match, forming a strap that is 1 inch (2.5 cm) wide. You should be folding about ½ inch (1.3 cm) under on both sides.

4. Press again and topstitch ⅛ inch (3 mm) in from the edge along both long edges of each strap with coordinating thread. Fold the short ends in about ¼ inch (6 mm) and top-stitch ⅛ inch (3 mm) from each edge.

5. Trace the row of books from the template onto one of the fabric C panels. Stitch the books with four strands of embroidery floss. Use a split stitch (page 5) for the outside of the book, backstitch for the pages and mouth, and French knots for the eyes.

6. Fold the top of the fabric B piece over ½ inch (1.3 cm) and press. Fold it over another ½ inch (1.3 cm) and press. Topstitch ⅛ inch (3 mm) from the edge with coordinating thread.

7. Place the embroidered panels along the raw edge of fabric B, right sides together. Make sure the embroidered books are upside down. Sew with a ¼-inch (6 mm) seam allowance, fold the piece flat, right sides out, and press. The books should then be right side up and positioned at the bottom of the tote. Repeat steps 6 and 7 to create the tote's back panel.

8. Fold the tote pieces lengthwise to find the center; fold each edge to the center again and place pins to mark the locations for the straps. You should have two pins about

4¼ inches (10.8 cm) from the outside edges. Pin the strap pieces there so that about 1½ inches (3.8 cm) overlaps the tote pieces. Sew the straps onto the bag using a square with an X in it for extra strength. Backstitch as much as possible for sturdiness.

9. Lay the tote pieces with attached straps right sides together and pin all the way around the sides and bottom. Sew the pieces together with a ¼-inch (6 mm) seam allowance. Backstitch at the beginning and end. For extra reinforcement, you can stitch around with a zigzag stitch in the seam allowance.

10. Turn the tote right side out!

FINISHED SIZE

- 14½ x 14 x 2¼ inches (36.8 x 35.6 x 5.7 cm)

MATERIALS

- 16 fat quarters: 2 white (sides, back, and bottom of tote and space above books), 1 light brown (bookshelf), 11 bright colors (books on shelf), 2 white with black text (lining and trim)
- Basic Sewing Kit (page 2)
- Masking tape (see note)
- ½ yard (45.7 cm) of fusible fleece
- Ruler
- 1¾ yards (1.6 m) of fuchsia cotton webbing, 1 inch (2.5 cm) wide
- NOTES: *All seam allowances are ¼ inch (6 mm) unless otherwise indicated.*

  Label pieces with masking tape as you cut fabric for the front of the tote.

PIECED BOOKSHELF TOTE

Stash a weeks-vacation-at-the-beach worth of books in this sturdy tote. The pieced book block is colorful and simple to create.

DESIGN BY CYNTHIA SHAFFER

16 FAT Quarters

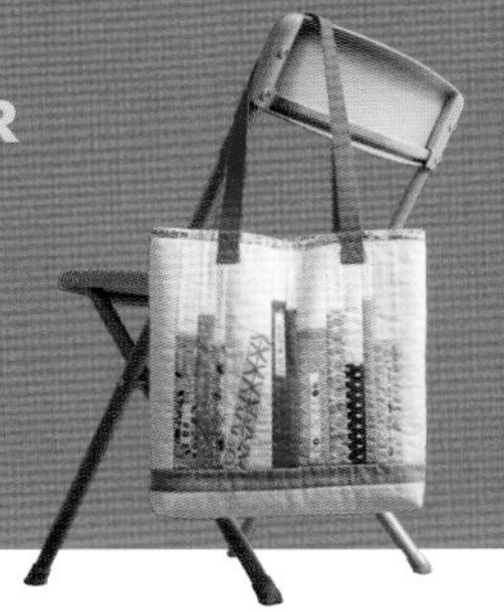

INSTRUCTIONS

1. Cut fabric as follows:

- Two pieces from the white fabric, 2½ x 12 inches (6.4 x 30.5 cm). These will be the side panels.

- One piece from the white fabric, 15½ x 3 inches (39.4 x 7.6 cm). This will be the bottom panel.

- One piece from the light brown fabric, 15½ x 1½ inches (39.4 x 3.8 cm). This will be the bookshelf.

- Book A: 1½ x 7 inches (3.8 x 17.8 cm); white fabric above book: 1 ½ x 5½ inches (3.8 x 14 cm).

- Book B: 1¼ x 8 inches (3.2 x 20.3 cm); white fabric above book: 1¼ x 4½ inches (3.2 x 11.4 cm).

- Book C: 1⅛ x 6½ inches (2.9 x 16.5 cm); white fabric above book: 1⅛ x 6 inches (2.9 x 15.2 cm).

- Book D: 1½ x 7¼ inches (3.8 x 18.4 cm); white fabric behind book: 2¾ x 12 inches (7 x 30.5 cm).

- Book E: 1¼ x 9 inches (3.2 x 22.9 cm); white fabric above book: 1¼ x 3½ inches (3.2 x 8.9 cm).

- Book F: 1 x 8½ inches (2.5 x 21.6 cm); white fabric above book: 1 x 4 inches (2.5 x 10.2 cm).

- Book G: 2 x 7¼ inches (5.1 x 18.4 cm); white fabric above book: 2 x 5¼ inches (5.1 x 13.3 cm).

- Book H: 1¼ x 8 inches (3.2 x 20.3 cm); white fabric above book: 1¼ x 4½ inches (3.2 x 11.4 cm).

- Book I: 1⅜ x 5¼ inches (3.5 x 13.3 cm); white fabric above book: 1⅜ x 7¼ inches (3.5 x 18.4 cm).

- Book J: 1 x 9 inches (2.5 x 22.9 cm); white fabric above book: 1 x 3½ inches (2.5 x 8.9 cm).

- Book K: 1¾ x 6½ inches (4.4 x 16.5 cm); white fabric above book: 1¾ x 6 inches (4.4 x 15.2 cm).

- One piece from the white fat quarter that measures 15 x 15¼ inches (38.1 x 38.7 cm). This is for the back of the tote.

- Two pieces from the white with black text fabric that measure 15 x 15¾ inches (38.1 x 40 cm) each. These pieces are for the lining.

- Two pieces from fusible fleece that measure 15 x 15¼ inches (38.1 x 38.7 cm) each.

2. Pin and stitch the short ends of book A to the corresponding white panel. Repeat for all the books except D.

3. Stitch all the book segments together, including the white panel for book D, in order.

4. Stitch the 2½ x 12-inch (6.4 x 30.5 cm) white side panels to the stitched book panel.

5. Stitch the 15½ x 1½-inch (39.4 x 3.8 cm) brown shelf to the bottom white tote piece, and then stitch this to the book panel.

6. Press under all sides of book D ¼ inch (6 mm) and then topstitch it to the book D white panel. Angle the book so that it looks like it is tipped toward the right.

7. Press the seams open.

8. Cut out narrow strips of the fabric with text or cut out strips from the selvedge edge, where the fabric information is printed. Zigzag appliqué (see page 4) these strips to a few of the book spines.

9. Following the manufacturer's instructions, fuse the fusible fleece to the back of the book tote front and to the back panel.

10. Place the book panel and the back panel together, right sides facing, and pin in place. Stitch the sides and the bottom, pivoting at the corners.

11. Press the side seams open. Create boxed corners (page 6) by flattening the bottom seam at the corner and align it with the side seam to create a point. Use a ruler and mark a line across the point, 1 inch (2.5 cm) from the point. Pin in place and machine-stitch across the point. Trim away the point fabric. Repeat for the other corner.

12. Turn the tote right side out.

13. With right sides facing, stitch the lining at the sides and the bottom, leaving a 4-inch (10.2 cm) opening along the bottom edge.

14. Press the side seams open. Repeat step 11 to create boxed corners.

15. Slip the tote into the lining right sides together. Pin and stitch around the top.

16. Pull the outer tote through the bottom opening in the lining. Fold the lining opening seam allowance in and machine-stitch the opening closed.

17. Roll the lining to the outside at the top edge and pin in place. Stitch in the ditch (see page 8) to keep the lining in place.

18. Cut two lengths of cotton webbing that measure 19 inches (48.3 cm) each.

19. Turn the ends of the straps under ½ inch (1.3 cm) and pin the straps to the outside of the tote, 3½ inches (8.9 cm) in from the sides and 1½ inches (3.8 cm) down from the top edge. Stitch the straps securely in place.

FINISHED SIZE

- 13 x 7¼ inches (33 x 18.4 cm)

MATERIALS

- 3 fat quarters: 1 of fabric A (medium-weight linen or similar), 1 of fabric B (patterned contrast for pockets and handles, 1 of fabric C (plain or patterned fabric for lining)
- Basic Sewing Kit (page 2)
- Scrap of fabric D (lightweight lining fabric for pockets)
- Cotton quilt batting
- Templates (page 156)

OVAL POCKET HANDBAG

Theretro style and two egg-shaped pockets of this high fashion handbag let you showcase a special fat quarter with eye-catching pizzazz.

DESIGN BY RUTH SINGER

3 FAT Quarters

INSTRUCTIONS

1. Cut fabric as follows:

- Two bag pieces from fabric A using the Body template.
- Two bag pieces from fabric C using the Body template.
- Two bag pieces from batting using the Body template.
- Two pocket pieces from fabric B using the Pocket template, placing the pattern carefully to make the most of the print, if appropriate.
- Two pocket pieces from fabric D using the Pocket template.
- Two handle pieces from fabric B, 18 x 2½ inches (45.7 x 6.4 cm) each.

2. Make the handles by folding each strip lengthwise with right sides together and press. Put a long piece of string or yarn inside, right up against the fold. Stitch across the yarn to hold it in place. Sew along the long side of the fabric strip with a ¼-inch (6 mm) seam allowance. Use the string to pull the tube right side out. Cut off the string and press the handle flat, with the seam to the back. Repeat for the second handle.

3. Prepare the pockets. Pin the fabric B and fabric D pocket pieces right sides together. Stitch around the hole, using a ¼-inch (6 mm) seam allowance. Trim the seam allowance by about half. Turn the lining

through the hole, then iron both pieces flat.

4. Working around the edge of the pockets, fold the fabric D and main fabric B edges underneath (to the lining side) ¼ inch (6 mm), tacking or basting as you go. Press flat.

5. Place the pocket on the fabric A front bag piece, 1½ inches (3.8 cm) from the top edge and side edge. Pin in place and machine-stitch all around the pocket, very close to the folded edge. Repeat with the other pocket. Remove basting if necessary.

6. Assemble the bag. Place one batting piece flat on your work surface, followed by the bag front, right side up, then the other bag front, right side down, and the other piece of batting on top.

7. Using a ⅝-inch (1.6 cm) seam allowance, sew around the sides and base of the bag, through all the layers, treating the bag and batting as one.

8. Trim the batting from the corners.

9. Create boxed corners (page 6). Open out the corner and press flat so the seams face each other. Mark 1 inch (2.5 cm) from the corner of the stitching (not from the edge of the seam allowance). Sew across, making sure that the stitched line is at right angles to the seam. Turn right side out.

10. Tack the handles onto the bag front and bag back using the template markings as guides; the raw edges should be together. Use a zigzag stitch and run two rows of stitching backward and forward near the raw edge to firmly attach the handles.

11. Make the lining in the same way (steps 6 through 9), including the boxed corners, but leave an opening in the bottom about 3 inches (7.6 cm) wide to turn the bag.

12. With the lining wrong side out and the bag right side out, place the bag inside the lining, tucking the handles inside. Sew around the top edge, using a ½-inch (1.3 cm) seam allowance. Turn through the opening in the lining.

13. Sew up the opening in the lining by hand or machine. Press the top edge.

FINISHED SIZE

- **Pocket: 11 inches square (27.9 cm)**

MATERIALS

- **1 fat quarter of ticking stripe**
- **Basic Sewing Kit (page 2)**
- **Matching thread**
- **Muslin or other fabric for pocket lining, 12 inches square (30.5 cm)**
- **Canvas tote bag, approximately 18½ x 16¼ inches (47 x 41.3 cm)**

PIECED POCKET TOTE

Take a store-bought tote from bland to beachy keen. Ticking takes center stage as a smartly pieced pocket design, though any striped fat quarter will work.

DESIGN BY BEKI LAMBERT

1 FAT Quarter

INSTRUCTIONS

1. Cut fabric as follows

- One 12 ¼-inch (31.1 cm) square from the fat quarter.
- Cut the square into fourths.

2. Arrange the four small squares so that the lines of squares form a diamond.

3. Sew the squares together using a ¼-inch (6 mm) seam allowance: sew the top two squares to make a rectangle, and then the bottom two squares to make a rectangle. Next, sew the rectangles together to make an 11¾-inch (30 cm) square.

4. Trim the lining fabric to fit the pieced square.

5. Position the lining fabric on the right side of your pieced square. If your lining fabric is a print or has a right and wrong side, make sure that the right side of the lining is facing the right side of the pocket. Pin in place.

6. Sew around the pocket using a ¼-inch (6 mm) seam allowance, leaving an opening of 4 inches (10.2 cm) at the center of one side.

7. Trim the corners of the pocket.

8. Turn the pocket right side out through the 4-inch (10.2 cm) opening. Smooth out the fabric, turn in the seam allowance along the opening, and press the pocket with an iron.

9. Position the pocket at the center of one side of the canvas tote. Make sure that the side with the opening is at either the bottom or one side.

10. Beginning on one side, sew the pocket to the tote down one side, across the bottom, and up the other side.

FINISHED SIZE
- approximately 3½ x 8 inches (8.9 x 20.3 cm)

MATERIALS
- 2 fat quarters: 1 for outer main (A), 1 for lining and outer accent (B)
- 3½-inch (8.9 cm) Flex frame
- Lightweight interfacing
- Pencil
- Pliers

FLEX FRAME SUNGLASSES POUCH
DESIGN BY KAYE PRINCE

2 FAT Quarters

INSTRUCTIONS

1. Cut as follows:

- Two pieces from fabric A, each measuring 4 x 7½ inches (10.2 x 19.2 cm)
- Two pieces from fabric B, each measuring 4 x 9½ inches (10.2 x 24.1 cm)
- Two pieces from Fabric B, each measuring 4 x 2½ inches (10.2 x 5.1 cm)
- Two pieces from interfacing, each measuring 4 x 7½ inches (10.2 x 19.2 cm)
- Two pieces from interfacing, each measuring 4 x 2½ inches (10.2 x 6.4 cm)

2. Following the directions for your interfacing, fuse the interfacing to the corresponding outer main and outer accents fabrics.

3. With right sides together, sew one outer accent piece to one outer main piece using a ¼-inch (6 mm) seam. Repeat with the other outer accent and outer main pieces.

4. Press the seam open and topstitch only along the outer main edge of the seam.

5. With right sides together, pin the lining pieces together and the outer pieces together.

6. Measure 2¼ inches (5.7 cm) down from the top of each the lining and outer pieces. Mark with your pencil. On the outer main pieces, this is directly at the seam where the main and accent pieces meet. Pin only below these marks.

7. Using a ¼-inch (6 mm) seam, sew along the three sides below your marks. On the lining piece, leave a 2-inch (5.1 cm) gap at the bottom. Trim the corners.

8. With right sides together, line up and pin one of the top free lining pieces to a top free outer piece. Repeat with the other top lining and outer pieces.

9. Using a ¼-inch (6 mm) seam, sew along the three sides of the top portion from mark to mark. Repeat

with second top portion. Trim away the excess fabric along all three sides, leaving only about ⅛-inch (3 mm) seam allowance.

10. Turn right side out through the opening in the bottom, being careful to push out the top flaps. Stitch the opening in the lining closed and push inside the pouch. Press.

11. Fold the top flaps in half so that the lining pieces are touching. The edges will line up at the accent seam when folded. Press.

12. Topstitch along this edge so that you are left with a channel for the flex-frame.

13. Feed the flex frame in through channel on both sides. When the flex frame is all of the way through, match the hinge, slide in the pin, and use the pliers to fold the end caps down.

ARROWHEAD CLUTCH

Go ahead and try to not love this clutch! From the bold color blocking to the row of triangles, this bag is pure hand-sewn style.

DESIGN BY KAYE PRINCE

3 FAT Quarters

FINISHED SIZE
• 9 x 10 inches (22.9 x 25.4 cm), unfolded

MATERIALS
• 3 fat quarters: 1 of fabric A for main clutch, 1 of fabric B for accent and zipper tabs, 1 of fabric C for lining
• Basic Sewing Kit (page 2)
• Fabric scraps for triangles
• Medium weight fusible interfacing
• Template (page 157)
• Cardstock
• 1 zipper, 9 inches (22.9 cm)
• Zipper foot

INSTRUCTIONS

1. Cut as follows:
- Two pieces from fabric A, each 7½ x 10 inches (19 x 25.4 cm).
- Two pieces from fabric B, each 4¼ x 10 inches (10.8 x 25.4 cm).
- Two more pieces from fabric B, each 1½ x 3 inches (3.8 x 7.6 cm).
- Two pieces from fabric C, each 11 x 10 inches (27.9 x 25.4 cm).
- Fabric scraps into five rectangles, each 1½ x 3 inches (3.8 x 7.6 cm).
- Two pieces from fusible interfacing, each 7½ x 10 inches (19 x 25.4 cm).
- Two more pieces from fusible interfacing, each 4¼ x 10 inches (10.8 x 25.4 cm).

2. Following manufacturer's instructions, fuse each cut piece of interfacing to its corresponding fabric A and fabric B pieces.

3. Trace five triangle templates onto cardstock. Cut out each cardstock template along the lines.

4. Pin one template to the wrong side of a 1½ x 3-inch (3.8 x 7.6 cm) scrap rectangle. Trim around the template, adding a ¼-inch (6 mm) seam allowance.

5. Fold the ¼-inch (6 mm) seam allowance on one side of the fabric down over the triangle template. Repeat with the remaining two sides until all of the fabric is folded nicely over the edges of the template.

6. Take a few stitches through one point of the triangle on the wrong side, being sure not to catch the cardstock template. Bring the thread across the seam allowance to the next point and repeat. Repeat until all three points are secure. Trim off the little nubbins at each point so that you are left with a nice-looking triangle. Repeat for the remaining four triangles.

7. Center the triangles along the right side of one 4¼ x 10-inch (10.8 x 25.4 cm) piece of fabric B, keeping in mind the ¼-inch (6 mm) seam allowance at the top and ½-inch (1.3 cm) seam allowances along the sides and bottom. Topstitch the triangles to the outer accent fabric.

8. With right sides together, sew one outer accent piece to each outer main piece using a ¼-inch (6 mm) seam allowance. Press seams open.

9. On the right side of each outer piece, topstitch on both sides of the seam.

10. Fold each 1½ x 3-inch (3.8 x 7.6 cm) piece of fabric B in half lengthwise and press. Fold each side edge in ¼ inch (6 mm) toward the wrong side and press again. Fold each rectangle over the end of the zipper and topstitch along the edge of the fabric (figure 1).

11. Lay the zipper facedown on the right side of one outer piece, lining up the zipper itself, not the zipper end pieces.

12. Lay one piece of fabric C, right side down, on top of the zipper. Line up the edges and pin all three layers together.

13. Using a zipper foot, stitch through all three layers.

14. Press both the outer piece and lining away from the zipper. Topstitch along the zipper edge of the fabric.

15. Lay the other side of the zipper, face up, on the second piece of fabric C (your Cs should be touching, right sides together).

16. Lay the second fabric A piece, right side down, on top of the zipper.

Line up the edges and pin all three layers together.

17. Repeating the steps above, sew the zipper in place and topstitch.

18. Open the zipper at least halfway and fold the pouch so that the outer pieces are right sides together and the lining pieces are right sides together. Pin. Trim off any excess from the zipper ends.

19. Using a ½-inch (1.3 cm) seam allowance, sew around the all of the edges, leaving a 3-inch (7.6 cm) opening along the bottom edge of the lining.

20. Trim the seam allowance at the corners and flip the clutch right side out using the opening in the lining. Use a turning tool to push out the corners. Press.

21. Sew closed the gap in the lining.

FINISHED SIZE

- **Lunch sack: 9 x 11½ inches (22.9 x 29.2 cm)**
- **Wrap bag: 5¼ x 8½ inches (13.3 x 21.6 cm)**
- **Snack bag: 6½ x 3 inches (16.5 x 7.6 cm)**

MATERIALS

- **3 fat quarters: 1 of fabric A for outer lunch sack, 1 of fabric B for lunch sack lining, 1 of fabric C for wrap and snack bags**
- **Basic Sewing Kit (page 2)**
- **Thread**
- **2 large buttons**
- **12-inch (30.5 cm) length of ribbon**
- **Ruler**

LUNCH SACK & SET

This lovely lunch bag set is designed to save all kinds of green. And we're pretty sure you'll be more inclined to eat your nutritious, delicious homemade lunch if it travels in a pretty package.

DESIGN BY JENNIFER RODRIGUEZ

3 FAT Quarters

INSTRUCTIONS

1. Cut fabric as follows:

- Two pieces from fabric A for the outer bag, each 10 x 17½ inches (25.4 x 44.5 cm).
- Two pieces from fabric B for the inner bag, each 10 x 17½ inches (25.4 x 44.5 cm).
- Two pieces from fabric C for the wrap bag, each 7 x 18 inches (17.8 x 45.7 cm).
- Two pieces from fabric C for the snack bag, each 8 inches square (20.3 cm).
- Two pieces from fabric C for the snack bag, each 2 x 8 inches (5.1 x 20.3 cm).

2. Pin the right sides of the two A pieces together and, with a ¼-inch (6 mm) seam allowance, sew both long edges and one short edge.

3. Pin the right sides of the two B pieces together and, with a ¼-inch (6 mm) seam allowance, sew both long edges. Sew one short edge, leaving a 2-inch (5.1 cm) opening in the center for turning.

4. Separately with both A and B, square up the bottom of the sack, drawing 45° angles on the sewn bottom of the sack. Sew along the line and clip the fabric close to the edge.

5. Place the inner bag, right side out, inside the outer bag's wrong side. Sew along the top of the sack with a

¼-inch (6 mm) seam allowance.

6. Pull the bag right side out through the opening from step 3, press the bag, and topstitch the top edge of the bag. Hand-sew the opening closed with a ladder stitch (page 5).

7. Sew one button centered on the front of the sack 4 inches (10.2 cm) up from the bottom.

8. Sew the other button on the back of the sack centered 2 inches (5.1 cm) down from the top. Securely hand-sew the ribbon underneath this button.

9. For the wrap bag, place both 7 x 18-inch (17.8 x 45.7 cm) fabric C pieces right sides together and pin. With a ¼-inch (6 mm) seam allowance, sew along the perimeter, leaving a 2-inch (5.1 cm) opening for turning.

10. Clip the corners of the fabric up to the stitching line and turn right side out.

11. Fold the fabric in half lengthwise. On one short edge, fold 1½ inches (3.8 cm) of fabric in. From the top of the fold, with a ¼-inch (6 mm) seam allowance, sew the edges together on both sides. Repeat the last step with a ⅛-inch (3 mm) seam allowance (see Figures 1 and 2).

Figure 1   **Figure 2**

12. Pull the fabric right side out. Your wrap bag will now close like an old-fashioned sandwich bag.

13. To make the snack bag, sew one of the 2 x 8-inch (5.1 x 20.3 cm) fabric scraps onto each of the 8-inch (20.3 cm) squares; they should now measure 8 x 9½ inches (20.3 x 24.1 cm).

14. Place the right sides together and pin. With a ¼-inch (6 mm) seam allowance, sew along the perimeter,

leaving a 2-inch (5.1 cm) opening for turning.

15. Clip the corners of the fabric up to the stitching line and turn it right side out.

16. Fold the fabric in half lengthwise. On one long edge, fold 1½ inches (3.8 cm) of fabric in. From the top of

the fold, with a ¼-inch (6 mm) seam allowance, sew the edges together on both sides. Repeat the last step with a ⅛-inch (3 mm) seam allowance.

17. Turn the fabric right side out. Your snack bag will now close like an old-fashioned sandwich bag.

QUILTS
& PILLOWS

FINISHED SIZE

- 62 x 63 inches (157.5 x 160 cm)

MATERIALS

- 20 fat quarters
- Basic Sewing Kit (page 2)
- Sizzix Big Shot Pro and Sizzix Bigz Pro Die-Tumbler 8 inches (20.3 cm) or Template (page 157)
- Straight edge or ruler
- Rotary cutter and mat
- 4 yards (3.7 m) of backing material
- 65 inches square (165.1 cm) of batting
- Coordinating thread for quilting
- ½ yard (45.7 cm) of fabric for binding

- NOTE: *All seam allowances are ¼ inch (6 mm) unless otherwise indicated.*

GROOVY VIBES QUILT

Give the traditional tumbler design a modern makeover by pairing the shapes and using bright and cheery coordinating fat quarters, one of which inspired the name of this quilt.

DESIGN BY AMY FRIEND

20 FAT Quarters

INSTRUCTIONS

1. Fold each fat quarter into quarters. Place the folded fat quarters on top of the die and run them through the cutter. You will cut four tumbler shapes from each fat quarter. If you do not have access to the die, you can cut your pieces using the template with a straightedge and rotary cutter.

2. Divide your fabrics into two color arrangements. Arrange the fabrics in pairs to create 10 columns of tumblers, with eight tumblers in each column. Alternate between color ways for each row.

3. Sew the first row of tumblers, together moving from left to right across the top row (see Figure 1). Press all seams to the right.

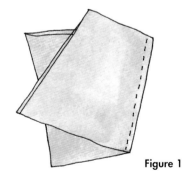

Figure 1

4. Sew the next row in the same fashion but press all seams to the left. Continue to alternate the direction in which you press the seams.

5. When all rows are complete, join the first two rows with right sides together. Pin where the seams meet.

The seam allowances should nest nicely if you correctly followed steps 3 and 4. Iron these horizontal seams open. Continue until the quilt top is complete.

6. Piece the backing if necessary.

7. Make your quilt sandwich and baste (page 8).

8. Quilt as desired. The quilt shown uses a series of free-motion "bubbles" in four sizes—4 inches (10.2 cm), 2½ inches (6.4 cm), 1½ inches (3.8 cm), and 1 inch (2.5 cm).

9. Square up the quilt, trimming the edges so that they are straight.

10. Cut your binding to 2¼ inches (5.7 cm) wide (page 10). Bind the quilt.

HOTHOUSE PILLOW SET

Grab your stack of bright floral fabrics to stitched up these paper-pieced pillows in cheery colors. Great to look at, they will pop in any setting.

DESIGN BY AMY FRIEND

9 FAT Quarters

FINISHED SIZE
• **15½ x 15 inches (39.4 x 38.1 cm)**

MATERIALS
• **9 fat quarters: 2 for backing of each pillow, 1 for leaves (for both pillows), 1 for flower centers (for both pillows), 1 for outer ring of petals (for both pillows), 2 for inner ring of petals (one for each pillow), 2 for background (one for each pillow)**
• **Basic Sewing Kit (page 2)**
• **Templates (page 158)**
• **½ yard (45.7 cm) of fusible fleece**
• **Coordinating thread for quilting**
• **Two 14-inch (35.6 cm) invisible zippers**
• **Two 16-inch (40.6 cm) pillow forms**
• **NOTE:** *All seam allowances are ¼ inch (6 mm) unless otherwise indicated.*

INSTRUCTIONS

1. Consult template on page 158 to find the following letters and the sections on the pattern to which they refer.

NOTE: for ease in piecing, fabric is often cut larger when used with paper-pieced patterns.

2. Cut fabrics as follows:

• Sections A1, C1: cut 16 pieces from leaf fabric, 4½ x 2½ inches (11.4 x 6.4 cm)
• Sections A2, C2: cut four squares on the diagonal from each of the two background fabrics, 3½ inches square (8.9 cm) (8 triangles total for each pillow)

• Sections A3, C3: cut 16 pieces, 6¾ x 3½ inches (17.1 x 8.9 cm)
• Sections B1, D1: cut eight squares on the diagonal, 3 inches square (7.6 cm)
• Sections B2, D2: cut 16 squares, 4 inches square (10.2 cm)
• Sections B3, D3: cut 16 pieces, 4 x 8 inches (10.2 x 20.3 cm)
• Sections B4, D4: cut eight squares on the diagonal, 5 inches square (12.7 cm)

3. Paper-piece (pages 6–7) all of the sections. Trim along the seam allowance line.

4. Each pillow is composed of four identical quadrants. To assemble one quadrant, join section C to section D.

Press seam up. Next, join section A and section B. Press seam down. Join these two sections on the diagonal to create one quadrant (see Figure 1).

Figure 1

5. To create each pillow front, join two quadrants and iron the center

seam to the left. Join the other two quadrants and iron the center seam to the right. Join the halves at the center seam. Iron this seam open.

6. Remove all foundation papers.

7. Cut two squares of fusible fleece to 16½ inches (41.9 cm). Starting at the center and pressing out, fuse each pillow front to a square of the fleece.

8. Quilt as desired.

9. Cut two backings each measuring 16½ inches square (41.9 cm).

10. Following the manufacturer's instructions, insert an invisible zipper at the bottom edge of each pillow. Stitch around the outside edge with right sides facing. Edge-finish seams and clip corners.

11. Turn the pillow covers right side out, press, and insert the 16-inch (40.6 cm) pillow forms.

FINISHED SIZE

- 17½ inches square (44.5 cm)

MATERIALS

- 3 fat quarters: 1 of fabric A, 1 of fabric B, 1 of fabric C
- 1 solid-color fat quarter for the cushion front (fabric D)
- 1 fat quarter for the cushion back (fabric E)
- Basic Sewing Kit (page 2)
- Rotary cutter and mat (optional)
- Ruler (optional)
- Sewing clips
- Zipper, 16 inches (40.6 cm)
- Zipper foot
- 2¼ yards (2.1 m) of cord for the piping, ½ inch (1.3 cm) wide
- 2¼ yards (2.1 m) of bias binding for the piping, 1½ inches (3.8 cm) wide
- Piping foot (optional)
- Serger (optional)
- Pillow form, 18 inches square (45.7 cm)
- **NOTES:** *Fat quarters should be small-scale prints or semisolids that work well together.*

All seam allowances are ¼ inch (6 mm) unless otherwise indicated.

STARBURST PILLOW COVER

Origami and fat quarters? Yes! Use three feature fabrics and some clever folds to create these stunning starbursts on linen.

DESIGN BY RUTH SINGER

5 FAT Quarters

INSTRUCTIONS

1. Using the rotary cutter, mat, and ruler or scissors (as preferred), cut fifteen 4-inch (10.2 cm) squares from fabrics A, B, and C; you will have 45 squares total.

2. Begin by folding a square in half diagonally; press. Fold again in half and press the fold, then unfold; the center line is marked.

3. Fold one side over as shown in Figure 1. Hold with a sewing clip. Fold it back on itself so the fold lies on the center line, like a paper airplane (see Figures 1 and 2). Repeat on the other side. Clip both edges.

Figure 1

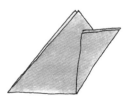

Figure 2

4. Keeping all the layers together, sew through from top to bottom (see Figure 3), catching all the layers. Keep the stitches small so the wings can spring back up. Repeat with the remaining 44 squares.

Figure 3

5. Cut an 18-inch square (45.7 cm) from fabric D. Mark dots to show the placement of the center of each starburst; essentially you're creating a grid of nine points, 5 inches (12.7 cm) in from each outer edge (see Figure 4).

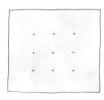

Figure 4

6. Position five airplane points together on the center mark to make a "starburst." Pin in place, adjusting to fit, so the edges all match up. Repeat for the other eight starbursts.

7. Hand-stitch each starburst in place, starting with the center point, then work around the star, catching the two edges of each airplane where it meets the next one. Stitch through the X stitch as well to hold the airplanes firmly to the backing (see Figure 5). Stitch the end tips down too, if necessary.

Figure 5

8. Cut an 18-inch (45.7 cm) square from fabric E. Fold and press to mark a center line. Mark 1 inch (2.5 cm) in from each edge along the line. Cut along the line and make a Y-shaped cut at the top and bottom, ⅜ inch (9.5 mm) wide. Fold the long edges and the little point at the top and bottom to the reverse side. Press.

This should produce a long rectangular box opening in the center of the cushion back.

9. Put the fabric right side up (folded-under seam allowances underneath) and position the zipper underneath so the teeth show through the opening. Baste the zipper in place, keeping the edges straight. Using a zipper foot, sew all around the box opening, through the zipper tape, close to the folded edge of the fabric. Take care when sewing across the short ends so you don't break the needle on the zipper teeth.

10. Make piping using the cord, bias binding, and zipper foot. Pin, then baste, the piping to the cushion front, along the seam line, clipping to go around the corners. Make the join by unpicking 1 inch (2.5 cm) of stitching and cutting away 1 inch (2.5 cm) of piping cord so the ends butt together. Fold under the lose end so you have a neat edge, then wrap the loose fabric over the other end of the piping cord. Baste in place.

11. Unzip the cushion back and place it facedown on top of the faceup cushion front. Using a piping foot or a zipper foot, sew as close to the piping as possible.

12. Trim the corners if required, and finish the inside seams using a zigzag stitch or serger. Turn right side out and insert the pillow form.

FINISHED SIZE

- 20 inches square (50.8 cm)

MATERIALS

- 4 fat quarters of different striped cotton: fabrics A, B, C, and D
- Basic Sewing Kit (page 2)
- Clear acrylic ruler
- Rotary cutter and mat
- ⅛ yard (11.4 cm) of solid-colored cotton fabric
- 1 piece of coordinating solid cotton fabric for the backing, 20 x 24 inches (50.8 x 61 cm)
- Coordinating machine-sewing thread
- 1 piece of cotton muslin, 20 x 24 inches (50.8 x 61 cm)
- Cotton batting
- 1 all-purpose zipper, 20 inches (50.8 cm) long
- 1 pillow form, 20 inches square (50.8 cm)

- NOTES: *All seam allowances are ¼ inch (6 mm) unless otherwise indicated.*

Press seams to one side, alternating sides where seams intersect.

STRIPED STRIPES PILLOW

Got a collection of striped fat quarters? Put them to work for you with this cheery courthouse steps pillow.

DESIGN BY MALKA DUBRAWSKY

4 FAT Quarters

INSTRUCTIONS

1. Cut fabrics as follows:

- Nine pieces from solid-colored fabric, each 1½ inches square (3.8 cm).
- Nine pieces from fabric A, each 1½ inches square (3.8 cm).
- Nine pieces from fabric A, each 1½ x 3½ inches (3.8 x 8.9 cm).
- Nine pieces from fabric A, each 1½ x 5½ inches (3.8 x 14 cm).
- Nine pieces from fabric B, each 1½ x 2½ inches (3.8 x 6.4 cm).
- Nine pieces from fabric B, each 1½ x 4½ inches (3.8 x 11.4 cm).
- Nine pieces from fabric B, each 1½ x 6½ inches (3.8 x 16.5 cm).

- Nine pieces from fabric C, each 1½ x 2½ inches (3.8 x 6.4 cm).
- Nine pieces from fabric C, each 1½ x 4½ inches (3.8 x 11.4 cm).
- Nine pieces from fabric C, each 1½ x 6½ inches (3.8 x 16.5 cm).
- Nine pieces from fabric D, each 1½ x 3½ inches (3.8 x 8.9 cm).
- Nine pieces from fabric D, each 1½ x 5½ inches (3.8 x 14 cm).
- Nine pieces from fabric D, each 1½ x 7½ inches (3.8 x 19 cm).
- Two pieces from coordinating cotton backing fabric, each 12 x 20 inches (30.5 x 50.8 cm).

2. Pin one 1½-inch (3.8 cm) solid-colored square and one fabric A 1½-inch (3.8 cm) square, right sides together, along one edge, and sew. Press seam to one side.

3. Pin one 1½ x 2½-inch (3.8 x 6.4 cm) fabric B strip to the sewn piece from step 1, right sides together, along the long edge and sew together. Press seam to one side.

4. Pin one 1½ x 2½-inch (3.8 x 6.4 cm) fabric C strip to the sewn group, right sides together, along the shared edge. Sew together. Press seam.

5. Pin one 1½ x 3½-inch (3.8 x 8.9 cm) fabric D strip to the sewn group, right sides together, along the long edge. Sew together. Press seam.

6. Using figure 1 as a guide, continue pinning, sewing, and pressing fabric A, B, C, and D strips together, adding strips of increasing lengths clockwise around the center square (see Figure 1).

Figure 1

7. Repeat steps 1 through 6 eight times to make a total of nine blocks.

NOTE: The pillow top is constructed of nine blocks put together in three rows.

8. Working with two blocks, rotate the orientation of one block so that fabric A strips appear to the left of the center block in one and to the right of the center block in the other.

9. Pin blocks together along fabric A strip sides. Sew together. Press seam.

10. Pin the third block to the sewn pair, right sides together, so that fabric C strips of the second and third block meet (see Figure 2).

Figure 2

NOTE: This order of construction applies to the top and bottom rows.

11. To construct the middle row blocks, orient and pin the first two blocks so that two fabric C strips meet. Sew together. Press seam.

12. With right sides together, pin the final middle row block so that the fabric A strips of the middle and third block meet. Sew together. Press seams.

13. Pin the top row to the middle row, right sides together, along a long edge. Sew together. Press seam.

14. Pin bottom row to middle row, right sides together, along a long edge. Sew together. Press seam.

15. Working on a flat surface, layer the muslin, wrong side facing up, batting, and pillow top, right side facing up.

16. Baste the layers (page 8).

17. Machine-quilt the layers and trim them flush.

NOTE: This sample was free-motion, machine-quilted with diagonal stitches sewn about ¼ inch (6 mm) apart.

18. Place one 12 x 20-inch (30.5 x 50.8 cm) backing piece wrong side up on an ironing surface. Press a ¼-inch (6 mm) fold along one long edge.

19. Turn under and press an additional 1-inch (2.5 cm) fold along same edge.

20. Pin the zipper, wrong side facing up, along the interior pressed, folded edge. Stitch the zipper in place along one side edge.

21. Place the second 12 x 20-inch (30.5 x 50.8 cm) backing piece, wrong side up on the ironing surface.

22. Press a ¼-inch (6 mm) fold along one long edge.

23. Pin the second backing piece, right side facing up, to the right side of the zipper along its unstitched edge.

24. Stitch the second backing piece to the zipper.

25. Working on a cutting surface, place the zippered backing and quilted top together, right sides facing.

26. Pin together. Trim edges flush.

27. Partially open the zipper for ease in turning.

28. Using a ¼-inch (6 mm) seam allowance, sew the backing and top together around all four sides.

29. Turn pillow right side out through zippered opening.

30. Press pillow. Insert form.

FINISHED SIZE

- 15 inches square (38.1 cm)

MATERIALS

- 3 fat quarters: 1 of fabric A for front, 1 of fabric B for appliqué, binding, and hanging tabs, 1 of fabric C for backing
- Basic Sewing Kit (page 2)
- Batting, 16 inches square (40.6 cm)
- Curved basting pins (optional)
- Fusible web, 10½ x 6 inches (26.7 x 15.2 cm)
- Template (page 159)
- Creasing marker (optional)
- Iron
- Sewing thread to match fabrics A and B
- Binding clips (optional)
- Size 8 perle cotton, to match fabrics A and B
- 14-inch (35.6 cm) thin dowel

- NOTE: *All seam allowances are ¼ inch (6 mm) unless otherwise indicated.*

ALL MY HEART MINI QUILT

With sweet details like heart appliqués and hand stitching, this simple mini quilt is at home on the wall or as a side table setting.

DESIGN BY JULIE ZAICHUK-RYAN

3 FAT Quarters

INSTRUCTIONS

1. Cut fabrics as follows:

- One piece from fabric A, 16 inches square (40.6 cm).
- One piece from fabric C, 16 inches square (40.6 cm).

2. Keeping the fabrics smooth, create a quilt sandwich with materials in this order: fabric C, right side down; batting square; fabric A, right side up. Secure with basting pins (or baste by hand) and quilt a diagonal grid pattern with lines 1 inch (2.5 cm) apart (or in another desired design, page 8).

3. Trim the quilt to 15 inches square (38.1 cm) to square up the edges after quilting. Set aside.

4. Trim the selvedge from fabric B and straighten all edges, then cut three 2½-inch strips along the width of the fabric (these should each be 20–21 inches / 51–53 cm long). These strips will be used for binding later. From the remaining fabric, cut two pieces 5½ x 3 inches (14 x 7.6 cm) for hanging tabs, then one large 10½ x 6 inch (26.6 x 15.2 cm) piece for appliqué. Apply fusible web to the appliqué piece, then

trace and carefully cut five hearts using the template.

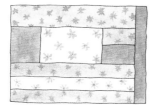

Figure 1

5. Using the marker, make a crease on your quilt from top to bottom, 4½ inches (11.4 cm) from the left side. Center the hearts on the crease so there is about 1 inch (2.5 cm) of space at the top and bottom, and ¾ inch (1.9 cm) between each heart. Alternatively, line the hearts up so that the center of each is 4½ inches (11.4 cm) from the left edge—measure carefully to be sure they are even and straight. Carefully apply the hearts to the quilt according to the fusible web instructions.

TIP: Press only one small spot of each heart with the tip of an iron, giving you the chance to double-check placement and make any adjustments before fully applying it to the quilt.

6. To make hanging tabs, fold one 5½ x 3-inch (14 x 7.6 cm) piece of fabric B in half, right sides and short ends together. Sew along the shorter 3-inch (7.6 cm) side, turn right side out, and press flat with the seam in

back. Fold in half again with seams together, and press. Repeat for the second tab. The tabs will now measure 2½ x 1½ inches (6.4 x 3.8 cm). With raw edges aligned, place the tabs along the top edge on the back of the quilt, about 2½ inches (6.4 cm) from the sides. Baste in place close to the top edge, then ladder-stitch (page 5) the folded ends down with thread to match the tabs.

7. To make the binding (pages 9–10), sew all three binding strips together, end to end, with right sides facing. Press seams open, then press in half with wrong sides together to make a long folded strip 1¼ inches (3.2 cm) wide.

8. With raw edges aligned, pin and then stitch the binding around the sides of the front of the quilt.

TIP: Do not allow a binding seam to land on a corner! Go back and start at a slightly different point if this happens.

9. Fold the binding around to the back and secure with binding clips or pins. Hand-stitch the folded edge to the quilt back as with the tabs in step 6, folding corners one side over the other as you reach them.

10. Burying your thread knots as you go, add a decorative line of running stitches (page 5) about ⅛ inch (3 mm) inside and outside the hearts as well as inside the binding. Use the perle cotton that matches the quilt inside the hearts and the one that matches the hearts on the quilt. You may choose to sew through all layers to add extra quilting, or sew across the top layer only as I did.

11. To hang your quilt, slide the dowel under the tabs. This will enable you to rest the dowel on nails or hooks.

CROSS ROADS LAP QUILT

With pieced crosses that make the most of three fat quarters, this lap quilt makes a fine (and cozy!) canvas for your favorite small cuts.

DESIGN BY MARILYN BUTLER

3 FAT Quarters

FINISHED SIZE

- 54 x 38 inches (137.2 x 96.5 cm)

MATERIALS

- 3 fat quarters for the quilt top: 1 of fabric A, 1 of fabric B, 1 of fabric C
- Basic Sewing Kit (page 2)
- 1⅔ yards (1.5 m) of fabric D for the background
- Three ½-yard (45.7 cm) pieces of fabric for the pieced quilt backing (optional)
- Cotton batting, 44 x 60 inches (1.1 x 1.5 m)
- ½ yard (45.7 cm) of fabric for the binding
- NOTE: *All seam allowances are ¼ inch (6 mm) unless otherwise indicated.*

INSTRUCTIONS

1. Cut fabric as follows:

- Two pieces from the long side of fabric A, each 2½ x 20 inches (6.4 x 50.8 cm).
- Seven pieces from the remaining 13-inch (33 cm) side of fabric A, each 2½ inches (6.4 cm) wide.
- Repeat above with fabric B and fabric C.
- Cut each 13-inch (33 cm) piece of fabric A, B, and C in half, for a total of 42 pieces, each 2½ x 6½ inches (6.4 x 16.5 cm).
- Six strips from background fabric D, each 2½ inches (6.4 cm) x width of fabric (WOF). Cut those

into 12 strips, each 2½ x 20 inches (6.4 x 50.8 cm).

- Two strips from background fabric D, each 4½ inches (11.4 cm) x WOF. Cut those into 12 pieces, each 4½ x 6½ inches (11.4 x 16.5 cm).

2. Sew one 20-inch fabric D background strip to one 20-inch fat quarter strip (A, B, or C), stitching the long side of the strips together. Sew a second 20-inch fabric D strip to the opposite side of the fat quarter strip.

3. Cut the finished strip set into eight pieces, each 2½ x 6 ½ inches (6.4 x 16.5 cm).

4. To create the "crossroads" rows, alternate and sew together (along the long edges) the eight 2½ x 6½-inch (6.4 x 16.5 cm) strip-set pieces you just made with seven 2½ x 6 ½-inch (6.4 x 16.5 cm) fat quarter pieces, working with the same fabric (A, B, or C) and beginning and ending with a pieced strip (see Figure 1).

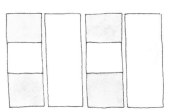

Figure 1

5. Sew a 4½ x 6½-inch (11.4 x 16.5 cm) background fabric D piece to each end of the row, stitching the long side.

The pieces you cut from each fat quarter are enough to complete two rows, so now make a second row identical to the one just finished.

Continue in the same way with the pieces you cut from the other two fat quarters and background fabric D.

6. Cut five strips from background fabric D, each 2½ x 38½ inches (6.4 x 97.8 cm), then cut two strips 4½ x 38½ inches (11.4 x 97.8 cm).

7. On your design wall or the floor, start at the top and lay down a 4½ x 38½ -inch (11.4 x 97.8 cm) piece of background fabric D; then lay a crossroads row below that, then a 2½

x 38½ -inch (6.4 x 97.8 cm) background fabric D strip. Repeat, ending with the second 4½ x 38½ -inch (11.4 x 97.8 cm) row on the bottom.

Play around with the arrangement of the crossroads rows. You have two rows from each fat quarter fabric to put in any order that is pleasing to you. Just be sure to have a background fabric D strip between each crossroads row.

8. For the optional quilt backing, cut two strips from fabric D, each 5 inches (12.7 cm) x WOF.

9. Decide on the placement of your ½-yard (45.7 cm) fabric backing pieces and the background fabric D strips sew them together, stitching along the long edges.

NOTE: For this sample, the designer alternated the backing pieces with the fabric D strips, creating horizontal stripes.

10. Make a quilt sandwich with the quilt top, cotton batting, and backing (see page 8). Pin or baste all layers in place. Quilt as desired (see page 8).

11. From the binding fabric, cut five strips 2¼ inches (5.7 cm) x WOF. Stitch the binding strips together end-to-end to make one long strip. Fold and press the binding strip in half, lengthwise, and bind your quilt (see pages 9–10).

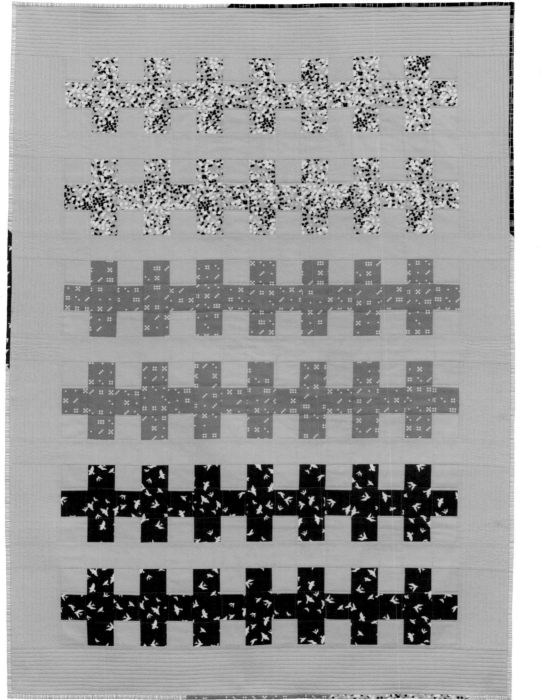

FINISHED SIZE
- 11 x 8 inches (27.9 x 20.3 cm)

MATERIALS
- 2 fat quarters: 1 of wood-grain pattern (fabric A), 1 of cream-colored solid (fabric B)
- Basic Sewing Kit (page 2)
- Drafting compass
- Brown embroidery floss
- Fiberfill
- **NOTE:** *All seam allowances are ¼ inch (6 mm) unless otherwise indicated.*

TREE TRUNK CUSHION

Great as a poof or a small stool, put your wood-grains to good use with this novelty pillow project. Even better: embroider or applique a set of "carved" initials.

DESIGN BY JENNIFER RODRIGUEZ

2 FAT Quarters

INSTRUCTIONS

1. Cut fabric A into two 9 x 19-inch (22.9 x 48.3 cm) pieces. Sew the short ends together to create a short, fat tube.

2. Draw two circles, 12 inches (30.5 cm) in diameter, on fabric B using the drafting compass and cut them out.

3. Lightly draw some irregular wood-grain circles on one of the fabric B circles. Thread the needle with two strands of brown embroidery floss and backstitch (page 5) the circle shapes.

4. With right sides together, pin the embroidered circle to the wood-grain tube. Sew the circle and tube together.

5. Pin the remaining circle to the other side of the wood grain tube. Sew the circle to the tube together, but leave a 2-inch (5.1 cm) opening.

6. Turn the pillow form right side out and gently press out the seams. Fill with polyester fiberfill.

7. Close the hole with a ladder stitch (page 5).

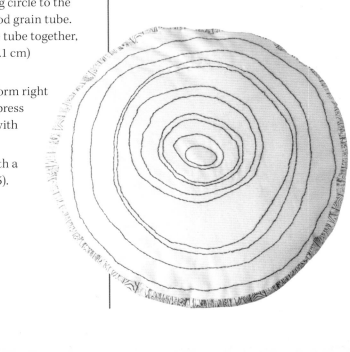

FINISHED SIZE

- 47 x 64 inches (1.2 x 1.6 m)

MATERIALS

- Various fat quarters (enough to cut 35 10-inch [25.4 cm] squares)
- Basic Sewing Kit (page 2)
- Rotary cutter, mat, and ruler (optional)
- Tape (optional)
- 1 flannel-backed tablecloth, at least 52 x 70 inches (1.3 x 1.8 m)
- 4 grommets, 1 inch (2.5 cm), and grommet kit
- Utility knife
- Hammer
- NOTE: *All seam allowances are ¼ inch (6 mm) unless otherwise indicated.*

PATCHWORK PICNIC BLANKET

Take your pretty creations outdoors! The grommets and vinyl increase this blanket's usability: spread it on the ground for a picnic or stake the corners and use it as a simple fabric tent in the yard.

DESIGN BY KATHLEEN WALCK

33-35 FAT Quarters

INSTRUCTIONS

1. Using a rotary cutter, mat, and ruler, cut the cotton fabric as follows:

   - 33 pieces, each 10 inches square (25.4 cm).
   - Four pieces, each 10 x 5 inches (25.4 x 12.7 cm).

2. Arrange these fabric squares into five columns in a staggered pattern so that the colors look best to you. Consider numbering your squares with tape to remember the order. Use the smaller pieces to fill in the second and fourth columns at the top and bottom.

3. Sew the squares in the first column of fabric, right sides together. Do the same for each subsequent row until you have all five columns sewn. Press all seams in the same direction.

4. Sew the columns together to make the blanket top. Press seams.

5. With right sides together, pin the blanket top to the vinyl tablecloth. Trim away any excess fabric from the tablecloth. Sew around the outside of the blanket, leaving an 8-inch (20.3 cm) opening on one side to turn it right side out. Trim off any extra fabric from the edges.

6. After turning the blanket right side out, lightly press the edges and hand-sew the opening closed. Topstitch ½ inch (1.3 cm) from the outside edge around the entire perimeter of the blanket.

7. For the grommeted corners, measure 1 inch (2.5 cm) in from each corner. Trace the inside of the grommet onto the blanket with chalk or an erasable marker. With a utility knife, slice an X inside that circle.

8. Push the male end of the grommet through the X and trim away any excess fabric. Place the female grommet part on top. Using the grommet kit, hammer the grommets into place.

HOME DECOR

FINISHED SIZE

- **17½ x 11½ x 4 inches (44.5 x 29.2 x 10.2 cm)**
  (Will vary depending on your ottoman's dimensions.)

MATERIALS

- **4 coordinating fat quarters**
- **Basic Sewing Kit (page 2)**
- **Footstool frame, 19¾ x 13¾ inches (50.2 x 35 cm)**
  with 6-inch (15.2 cm) legs
- **Wood paint for the footstool (optional)**
- **Sandpaper (optional)**
- **Rotary cutter and mat**
- **Square ruler**
- **4-inch-thick (10.2 cm) high-density upholstery foam,**
  12 x 17¾ inches (30.5 x 45.1 cm) (or two pieces,
  2 inches [5.1 cm] thick, same dimensions)
- **Plywood, 12 x 17¾ inches (30.5 x 45.1 cm)**
- **Staple gun and staples**

COTTAGE FOOTSTOOL

Cover an old ottoman with simple pieced stripes in a favorite fabric line. And then, as an optional step, move to a sunny beachside locale.

DESIGN BY VICK GUTHRIE

INSTRUCTIONS

1. Prepare the base of your footstool by painting with wood paint and allowing it to dry. If you are refurbishing an old footstool, first sand it down, then paint or leave the wood bare, as desired.

2. Cut strips from fat quarters across the widest part. Think about how you'd like to arrange these pieces from different fabrics:

- 7¼ inches (18.4 cm) wide.
- 3¼ inches (8.3 cm) wide.
- 4 inches (10.2 cm) wide.
- 4¼ inches (10.8 cm) wide.
- 5¼ inches (13.3 cm) wide.
- 2¼ inches (5.7 cm) wide.
- 8¼ inches (21 cm) wide.

3. Set the stitch length shorter on your sewing machine; the seams will be taking a lot of strain so we want to make sure they are held together well. Using a ¼-inch (6 mm) seam allowance, sew the strips together in an arrangement you are happy with to form a rectangle that measures 34½ x 22 inches (87.6 x 55.9 cm).

4. Press all of the seams neatly in one direction.

5. To make the cushion pad, place the rectangle of fabric facedown on your table or floor. In the very center, place the foam pad(s) and then the plywood on top.

6. Starting on the longer sides, bring one edge of the fabric up over the side of the foam and over to the back of the plywood. Pull firmly, but be careful because you can misshape the fabric if you pull on it too hard. I recommend pulling it just enough so that the corner of the foam is slightly rounded. Staple the fabric a few times onto the plywood right in the center. Repeat this for the opposite side.

7. Repeat step 6 for the two shorter ends. Once you have some staples in the center of each side, move around each side of the pad, pulling the fabric evenly and stapling from the center outward toward the corners. Stop regularly to turn it over and check that it looks even all the way around and that the fabric strips are straight.

Stop 2 inches (5.1 cm) from each corner on all sides.

8. To achieve nice and neat corners, fold each corner in toward the shorter sides of the footstool so you have a neat triangle, the same way you would if you were wrapping a present. Play with the fabric to get it as neat and crisp as possible, then bring it to the underside and staple securely. Repeat this for all corners.

9. Turn your cushion pad right side up; it should slot perfectly into your footstool base. Now put your feet up (sorry, I couldn't resist!) and enjoy your hard work!

TIP: When stapling the fabric, it's handy to have someone else to hold it still for you—it's tricky to maneuver, staple, and hold the pad still all on your own at the same time!

QUILTED FRAME

Over a mirror or a teeny chalkboard, this pieced frame is the picture of cheer. Grab two favorite fat quarters, some foam board, and you're on your way.

DESIGN BY JESSICA FEDIW

2 FAT Quarters

INSTRUCTIONS

1. Cut 24 5-inch (12.7 cm) squares, 12 from fabric A and 12 from fabric B.

2. Place one A square on top of a B square, right sides facing, then draw a line diagonally from one corner to the next. Sew together ¼ inch (6 mm) away from drawn line on both sides.

3. Cut the squares in half right on the diagonal line that was drawn. Open the shapes and iron the new half-square triangles.

4. Repeat steps 2 and 3 for the remaining squares.

5. Place the squares (see Figure 1).

Figure 1

6. Sew all the squares together. Start on one side and work your way around.

7. Place backing fabric on your worktable. Top with quilt batting, then place the fabric squares, right side up, on top of that. Pin together.

NOTE: The half-triangle-squares piece will be smaller than the fabric and batting.

8. To quilt the layers, sew around the inner square first, as close to the edge as possible. Then sew around the square again about 1 inch (2.5 cm) from that line. Sew rows around until you reach the edge. Sew one last time around the very edge of the square.

9. Trim excess backing fabric and batting from the sides and from the middle so they are each the same size as the half-triangle squares.

10. Cut out a 16½-inch (41.9 cm) square from the foam board using the utility knife. Cut a 10½-inch-square (26.7 cm) hole from the middle.

11. Place the quilted frame on top of foam board, right side facing up. Center it so the same amount of

fabric goes over the edge on all sides. Hot-glue the fabric piece to the foam board.

12. Wrap the excess side fabric over the sides of the foam board and glue in place. For the middle area, you will need to cut straight down toward each corner of the fabric until you are

¼ to ½ inches (6 mm to 1.3 cm) away from the foam board. Then fold those pieces under and glue in place.

13. Place the frame face up on top of poster board. Trace the outer and inner edges with a pencil. Cut out the traced portion on the inside of the pencil line. Place this square on the

back of frame and see if it needs any extra trimming. You should not see any of the poster board from the front. Glue on to the back to cover all the raw edges.

14. If desired, hot-glue a sawtooth hanger at the center top of the poster board.

FINISHED SIZE

- 3 to 6 inches (7.6 to 15.2 cm) in diameter

MATERIALS

- 14 fat quarters: 11 in coordinating green prints, 3 in coordinating brown prints
- Basic Sewing Kit (page 2)
- White craft glue
- 4 wood embroidery hoops, 6 inches (15.2 cm) in diameter
- 4 wood embroidery hoops, 5 inches (12.7) in diameter
- 5 wood embroidery hoops, 4 inches (10.2 cm) in diameter
- 3 wood embroidery hoops, 3 inches (7.6 cm) in diameter
- Template (page 159)
- Fusible web, 4 inches square (10.2 cm)
- Scrap of red fabric, 4 inches square (10.2 cm)
- White embroidery floss
- Green chalk

HOOP TREE

Hoop up your favorite fat quarters and scraps to create this cute tree. Or use the same technique to make a festive Christmas tree or a woodland mushroom.

DESIGN BY CYNTHIA SHAFFER

14 FAT Quarters

INSTRUCTIONS

1. Place a 6-inch (15.2 cm) inner hoop on the wrong side of a green-patterned fat square and trace around the hoop with a pencil.

2. Cut the circle 1 inch (2.5 cm) outside the traced line.

3. Center the circle on the inner hoop and place the outer hoop on top; push the hoops together.

4. Flip the hoop to wrong side and trim away the excess fabric, close to the wooden hoop.

5. Apply a small amount of white glue all around the cut fabric edge and press it to the hoop. Set aside to dry.

6. Repeating steps 1 through 5, stretch green fat quarters on the following hoops:

- Three 6-inch (15.2 cm) hoops
- Four 5-inch (12.7 cm) hoops
- One 4-inch (10.2 cm) hoop
- Three 3-inch (7.6 cm) hoops

7. Repeat steps 1 through 5 and stretch brown fat quarters on three 4-inch (10.2 cm) hoops.

8. Place a 3-inch (7.6 cm) inner hoop on the wrong side of a green-patterned fat square and trace around the hoop with a pencil.

9. Cut the circle 1 inch (2.5 cm) outside the traced line.

10. Trace the Apple template onto the paper side of the fusible web.

11. Iron the fusible web onto the wrong side of the red fabric, and then cut out the apple.

12. Following the manufacturer's directions, center the apple on the green circle, and fuse.

13. Hand-stitch around the apple with embroidery floss and a long running stitch (page 5).

14. Center the circle on the inner hoop, then place the outer hoop on top and push the hoops together.

15. Flip the hoop to wrong side and trim away the excess fabric, close to the wooden hoop.

16. Apply a small amount of white glue all around the cut fabric edge and press it to the hoop. Set aside to dry.

17. Arrange the hooped fabric to look like a tree with the brown hoops as the trunk and the green ones as the foliage. The one green hoop with the appliquéd apple can lie on the ground to the right of the trunk.

18. Use green chalk to outline the tree. Make the outline thicker and thinner in places to add a little interest.

FINISHED SIZE
- 9½ x 3½ inches (24.1 x 8.9 cm)

MATERIALS
- 3 fat quarters in coordinating colors and prints
- Basic Sewing Kit (page 2)
- Templates (page 162)
- Lightweight fusible interfacing, 10 inches square (25.4 cm)
- Polyester fiberfill
- Pencil with eraser

- **NOTE:** *All seam allowances are ¼ inch (6 mm) unless otherwise indicated.*

FABRIC BIRDS

Brighten your home with a flock of fabric friends. These guys just may be the sweetest stash busters ever.

DESIGN BY CYNTHIA SHAFFER

3 FAT Quarters

INSTRUCTIONS

1. Fold a fat quarter in half, right sides together, lengthwise. Pin template A on the fabric and cut out. You now have one opposite pair for the upper bird. Transfer all markings.

2. Fold another fat quarter in half, right sides together, lengthwise. Pin template B on the fabric and cut out. You will now have one opposite pair for the under bird. Transfer all markings.

3. Fold another fat quarter in half, right sides together, lengthwise. Pin template C onto the fabric and cut out. Cut out a second pair of template C on this fabric. You will now have two opposite pairs of wings.

4. Fold the lightweight interfacing in half, right sides facing, and cut out two pairs of template C.

5. Pin the top edge of the upper bird together and start stitching at the end near the tail, continue to the top of the head and pivot at the tip of the beak. Continue stitching the under neck until you reach the mark at the base of the neck, then backstitch. Snip little wedges out of the seam allowance at the head curve and snip into the seam allowance at the under-neck area.

6. Pin the under bird pieces together along the edge with the marks, then stitch. Place double pins at those marks and do not sew in between

the double pins. This opening allows you to turn the bird right side out after all the machine-stitching is complete.

7. Pin the upper bird to the under bird, then start stitching at the point where the neck and under bird intersect, continue down to the tail, pivoting at the corners of the tail, and continue up to the neck and under-bird intersection. Backstitch at the beginning and the end of this seam.

8. Clip the corners of the tail.

9. Stuff the bird with polyester fiberfill. Use the eraser end of a pencil to poke and shove the fiberfill into the beak and the tail.

10. Hand-stitch the belly opening closed.

11. Fuse the interfacing to the wrong sides of an opposite pair of wings. Pin the other pair of wings onto the interfacing and machine-stitch around the perimeter, close to the cut edge.

12. Hand-tack the wings onto the bird at the transferred markings.

FINISHED SIZE
• **Two panels: 21 x 63 inches (53.3 cm x 1.6 m) each**

MATERIALS
• **13 fat quarters: 4 of fabric A, 3 of fabric B, 3 of fabric C, and 2 of fabric D for patchwork (The designer used gray, yellow, aqua, and black, respectively.); 1 of fabric E for the curtain casing**
• **Basic Sewing Kit (page 2)**
• **Ruler**
• **Rotary cutter and mat**
• **18 inches (45.7 cm) of grosgrain ribbon, ½ inch (1.3 cm) or wider**

CHEVRON CURTAINS

The loveliness of half square triangles is on full display in these patchwork curtains. Once closed, the triangles create a cool chevron effect.

DESIGN BY LINDSAY CONNER

13 FAT Quarters

INSTRUCTIONS

1. Cut fabric as follows:

• One piece of fabric E into two pieces for the curtain casing, each 22 x 9 inches (55.9 x 22.9 cm).

• From the remaining fat quarters, cut one 18-inch (45.7 cm) square. Set aside the 4 x 18-inch (10.2 x 45.7 cm) scraps for another project.

2. Pair up the squares into six sets of two, which will become your half-square triangles. For example, I used 1 pair of fabrics B and D, 1 pair of fabrics C and D, 2 pairs of fabrics A and B, and 2 pairs of fabrics A and C.

3. Stack one pair of 18-inch (45.7 cm) squares with right sides facing and pin in place around the perimeter. On the wrong side of the lighter fabric, mark a diagonal line from corner to corner. Repeat to draw a line connecting the other corners until you have a large X going through the square.

4. With the X facing up, stitch ¼ inch (6 mm) to the left and right of one marked line. Repeat with the other marked line, for a total of four stitched lines.

5. Cut the block into four equal quadrants with your ruler and rotary cutter (see Figure 1).

Figure 1

6. For each of the four quadrants, use your ruler and rotary cutter to slice along the diagonal lines you marked in step 3 (see Figure 2 on page 106). This yields eight half-square triangles. Press the seams open, and trim each block to 8 inches square (20.3 cm).

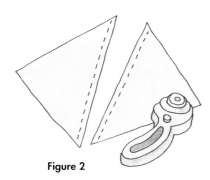

Figure 2

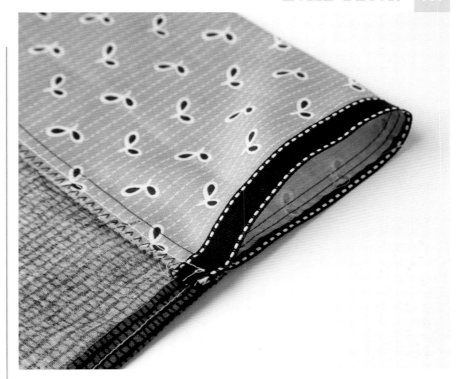

TIP: Use a square ruler and a rotary cutter with a 45° diagonal line for accurate trimming.

7. Repeat steps 3 through 6 with the other pairs of 18-inch (45.7 cm) squares to make a total of 48 half-square triangles.

8. Arrange the half-square triangles as pictured to make two curtain panels. In this sample, all of the gray and black triangles point up, while the yellow and aqua triangles point down. Pin and stitch the half-square triangles together using a ¼-inch (6 mm) seam allowance.

TIP: For accurate points, carefully pin the blocks together at each half-square triangle intersection. Another trick is to sew a small tack through each seam before joining together all the blocks in a row. This way, you can easily rip out the stitches and try again if the piecing isn't accurate.

9. Press the left, bottom, and right edges of each panel in ⅛ inch (3 mm) and then another ⅛ inch (3 mm). Topstitch in place to finish the raw edges.

10. Use the long fabric A rectangles from step 1 to finish the top of each curtain panel and add the curtain casing. Press one 9-inch (22.9 cm) side under ⅛ inch (3 mm) and then another ⅛ inch (3 mm). Topstitch to finish the raw edge; repeat with the other fabric A rectangle. If you need more length to finish the second edge, stitch grosgrain ribbon on the raw edge to finish. Repeat.

11. Press each fabric E rectangle in half lengthwise with wrong sides together (right sides facing out) to create the casing. Pin the raw edge of one folded rectangle against the right side of one curtain panel. Stitch ½ inch (1.3 cm) from the raw edge. Seal the raw edges together with a wide zigzag stitch or serger. Flip the curtain over and topstitch along the patchwork, ⅛ inch (3 mm) from the top casing. Repeat with the other panel.

FINISHED SIZE

- **Makes 6 coasters, each 4½ inches square (11.4 cm)**

MATERIALS

- **3 fat quarters: 1 of fabric A for coaster top, 1 of fabric B for backing, 1 of fabric C for binding**
- **Basic Sewing Kit (page 2)**
- **1 piece of batting, 10 x 15 inches (25.4 x 38.1 cm)**
- **Templates (page 162)**
- **Fusible web**
- **Fabric scraps for letters**
- **Black thread for sketchy appliqué**
- **White thread for quilting**

CHEERS COASTER SET

Throw a handmade celebration . . . and don't forget the coasters. This project is the perfect excuse to practice freeform stitching.

DESIGN BY KAYE PRINCE

3 FAT Quarters

INSTRUCTIONS

1. Cut fabric as follows:

- Six pieces from fabric A, each 4½ inches square (11.4 cm).
- Six pieces from fabric B, each 4½ inches square (11.4 cm).
- Six strips from fabric C, each 1¼ x 22 inches (3.2 x 55.9 cm).
- Six pieces from the batting, each 4½ inches square (11.4 cm).

2. Using a pencil, trace the letter templates onto the paper side of the fusible web. Cut around each fusible letter, leaving a small amount of overhang.

3. Following the manufacturer's directions, fuse each letter to the wrong side of the fabric scraps.

4. Cut out each letter along the original drawn lines.

5. Remove the paper back from each letter and, following the manufacturer's directions, center and fuse each letter (glue side down) to the right side of the coaster front squares.

6. Using the thread, stitch around each letter, being sure to catch all of the edges. For an even "sketchier" look, you can go around each letter a couple of times.

7. For each coaster, layer the backing, batting, and coaster top. Quilt as desired.

8. Use fabric C to create binding strips, and bind each coaster (pages 9–10). The finished binding is ¼ inch (6 mm).

FABRIC BASKETS

Use your stash fabric and get organized. Made with simple rectangles and in two sizes, these fabric baskets are as charming as they are useful. When your friends see these gorgeous fabric creations, they'll wonder what trendy store sells them.

DESIGN BY JENNY BARTOY

3 FAT Quarters

FINISHED SIZES

- Smaller basket: 4½ x 3¾ x 5½ inches (11.4 x 9.5 x 14 cm) plus 2-inch (5.1 cm) flap
- Larger basket: 5½ x 4 x 7 inches (14 x 10.2 x 17.8 cm) plus 2½-inch (6.4 cm) flap

MATERIALS

- 3 fat quarters: 1 of fabric A for small basket (for both interior and exterior), 2 of fabric B for large basket (one for interior, the other for exterior of basket)
- Basic Sewing Kit (page 2)
- 1 piece of batting, 10 x 17 inches (25.4 x 43.2 cm)
- 1 piece of batting, 12½ x 20½ inches (31.8 x 52.1 cm)
- Coordinating thread

INSTRUCTIONS

1. Cut your fabrics as follows:

   - Two rectangular pieces from fabric A, each 10 x 17 inches (25.4 x 43.2 cm).
   - Two rectangular pieces, one from each piece of fabric B, 12½ x 20½ inches (31.8 x 52.1 cm).

2. Make a pocket for each size basket. Layer the quilt batting on the wrong side of the fabric you've chosen for the outside of the basket. Fold right sides together (fabric folded on the inside, batting on the outside). Your folded fabric should measure 8½ x 10 inches (21.6 x 25.4 cm) for the smaller (fabric A) and 10¼ x 12½ inches (26 x 31.8 cm) for the larger (fabric B) baskets. Pin the edges together. Using a ¼-inch (6 mm) seam allowance, sew along one long edge and the bottom. The top remains open, creating a simple pocket.

3. Create a flat bottom for each size basket by boxing the bottom corners. With fabric wrong side out, match the side and bottom seams of one corner to create a flat point. Pin the layers together. Measure 2 inches (5.1 cm) for the smaller basket and 2½ inches (6.4 cm) for the larger basket from the tip of the point, and draw a perpendicular line with a fabric marker. Stitch along that line. Trim the excess fabric ¼ inch (6 mm) from the seam. Repeat with the other corner. Turn right side out.

4. Repeat steps 2 and 3 for the remaining fabric rectangles, minus the quilt batting. This fabric will be on the inside of the baskets and show on the folded edge.

5. Keep the second pocket wrong side out. Insert the first pocket, right side out, into it. Match seams and edges. Pin the layers all the way around the top.

6. Leaving a 4-inch (10.2 cm) opening, stitch all around the top. Backstitch at the start and end to secure your stitches.

7. Turn your basket inside out through the opening. Press all seams. Shape your basket by stuffing the interior layer into the exterior layer and smoothing them together.

8. Press in and pin fabric layers at the opening. Topstitch along the top of the basket, ⅛ inch (3 mm) from the edge, thereby stitching the opening closed.

9. Fold the top of the basket over. Your basket is now ready to use.

WEARABLES

FINISHED SIZE

- **31 x 16½ inches (78.7 x 41.9 cm)**

MATERIALS

- **8 fat quarters: 4 for outer side, 4 for inner side (see note below)**
- **Basic Sewing Kit (page 2)**
- **Coordinating thread**
- **Rotary cutter and mat**
- **NOTES:** *All seam allowances are ¼ inch (6 mm). Press seams to one side, alternating sides where seams intersect.*

  The designer used two fat quarters of the same color for both the outer and inner cowl fabrics, but you could do them all differently if you would like.

INFINITY COWL

Why should knitters have all the fun? Perfect for warmer months, this smart and stylish design will dress up your outfit with flattering fat quarters you can wear.

DESIGN BY SHANNON COOK

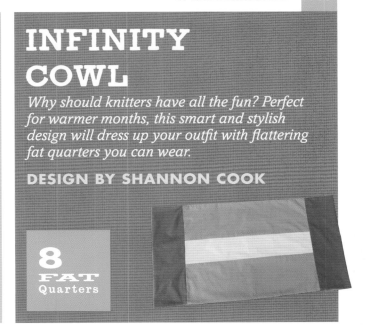

8 FAT Quarters

INSTRUCTIONS

1. Choose the color palette and fabrics for your two outer cowl and two inner cowl fat quarters.

2. To create the center panel, cut fabrics as follows:

- Two pieces 18 x 8¼ inches (45.7 x 21 cm) from your mid-tone fat quarters; these are the top and bottom strips of the center panel.
- One piece 18 x 6½ inches (45.7 x 16.5 cm) from your light-tone fat quarter; this piece is the center strip of the center panel.

3. With right sides facing, pin and sew the top strip to the middle strip along the long edge. Trim and press

your seam allowance toward the darker fabric. See Figure 1 for reference.

4. Now sew the bottom strip to the middle strip, with right sides facing. Trim and press your seam allowance toward the darker fabric.

5. With right sides facing each other, pin and sew the center panel to one of your outer fat quarters. Repeat with your other fat quarter, this time sewing along the other side edge.

6. Repeat the above steps, this time using your chosen fat quarters for the inner cowl portion.

7. You should now have two long strips of fabric comprised of three fat

quarters each (two solids and one pieced).

8. Lay the strips on top of each other and make sure that they are the same length and height and also that the center panels are the same size. You will need to be able to match these up in the next steps

9. Place the outer cowl and the inner cowl pieces with right sides facing and pin along the long edge, taking care that the center panels start and end at the exact same spots. Sew along this edge (see Figure 1 on page 115). Trim and press the seam allowance toward the darker fabric.

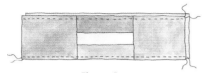

Figure 1

10. Repeat step 9, this time sewing along the other long edge. Your cowl will now look like a tube open at both ends.

11. Turn the cowl right side out and press. Lay the short ends together and match the center panel seams together. Pin the ends together where the seams meet, connecting your tube to create one continuous loop. Working your way up, continue to pin the edges of the ends together, keeping the raw edges of your seam hidden on the inside of the cowl. You won't be able to pin across the whole way (see Tip). You will be sewing next along the inside of the cowl, but your cowl will still be right side out (see Figures 2 and 3).

12. Starting where the seams meet for the center panel, sew along with a straight stitch slowly and carefully, taking care to not sew through the rest of your cowl. Continue doing this evenly, moving across the circle until you can't sew anymore; you will have approximately 4 to 5 inches (10.2 to 12.7 cm) left unsewn.

13. With the right side facing out, hand-stitch the opening closed using an invisible stitch.

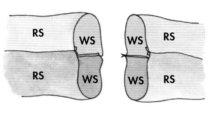

Figure 2

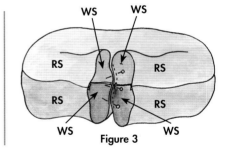

Figure 3

TIP: The cowl should stay three-dimensional, meaning that when you go to stitch the cowl ends, you are going to essentially seal the circles together, instead of just sewing them flat and straight across. In the following steps, it is important to make sure you are not sewing through other parts of your cowl.

FUNKY SCRUNCHY HEADBAND

Turn a set of three bright, fun fat quarters into a handy headband, perfect for taming your locks in style.

DESIGN BY JESSICA FEDIW

3 FAT Quarters

FINISHED SIZE
• 22 inches (55.9 cm) around

MATERIALS
• 3 fat quarters: 1 each of fabric A, fabric B, and fabric C in coordinating fabrics for elastic casings
• Basic Sewing Kit (page 2)
• 61½ inches (1.6 m) of elastic, ¼ inch (6 mm) wide
• Safety pin
• Heavy-duty sewing-machine needle (optional)
• 1 piece of scrap fabric, 2½ x 4 inches (6.4 x 10.2 cm)
• **NOTE:** *All seam allowances are ¼ inch (6 mm) unless otherwise indicated.*

INSTRUCTIONS

1. Cut two 2 x 14-inch (5.1 x 35.6 cm) rectangles from each fat quarter (six pieces total).

2. Cut three pieces of elastic, each 20½ inches (52.1 cm) long.

3. Sew the 2 x 14-inch (5.1 x 35.6 cm) pieces together in the following order to create three fabric strips:

• Strip 1: fabrics A-B-C.
• Strip 2: fabrics C-A-B.
• Strip 3: fabrics B-C-A.

4. Fold each strip in half along the long edge, right sides 'facing, and press.

5. Sew each strip down the long edge, leaving the two short ends open.

6. Turn each strip right side out; a turning tool makes this easy. Press flat so that the seam is in the middle of one side.

7. Attach the safety pin to one end of a piece of elastic. Thread the pinned end through one of the casings. Pull to bring the non-pinned end to the edge of fabric opening and sew in place.

8. Line up the pinned elastic end with the fabric opening on the other

side after removing the safety pin. Sew in place. The fabric will be bunched up at this point.

9. Repeat steps 7 and 8 for the remaining casings and elastic.

10. Place the three pieces together so the ends overlap at an angle, all the seams are underneath, and the strands are in same order as in step 3. Sew the ends together.

TIP: You might need to use a heavy-duty sewing-machine needle if you are having trouble sewing through all the layers.

11. Repeat step 10 for the other side of the fabric ends. Straighten out any twisting that might have occurred.

12. Place one end slightly over the other and sew the headband together.

13. Take the scrap fabric and fold two opposite sides in ¼ inch (6 mm), wrong sides facing. Press and sew in place.

14. Turn the two remaining edges in ¼ inch (6 mm) as well, wrong sides facing. Iron and sew in place.

15. Wrap the scrap fabric piece around the headband ends that were just sewn together so that it overlaps them as much as possible. The overlapping seam should be facing the inside of the headband. Sew down each side of fabric to hold it in place (see Figure 1).

Figure 1

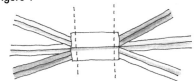

FINISHED SIZE

- Use a denim skirt that already fits you.

MATERIALS

- 8 fat quarters (or scraps): 1 turquoise, 1 light blue, 1 green, 1 light green, 1 mustard, 1 orange, 1 brown, 1 red*
- Basic Sewing Kit (page 2)
- Fusible web, ¼ yard (22.9 cm)
- Template (page 160)
- Skirt, approximately 19 inches (48.3 cm) long

- **NOTE:** *Use the same fat quarter for all your triangles if you like.*

RAINBOW CHEVRON SKIRT

Homemade doesn't have to mean from scratch. Revitalize and upcycle a denim skirt by adding a column of rainbow chevron appliqués. A single color fabric will work too, if rainbows aren't your thing.

DESIGN BY CYNTHIA SHAFFER

8 FAT Quarters

INSTRUCTIONS

1. Following manufacturer's instructions for the fusible web, cut eight rectangles that measure 5 x 4 inches (12.7 x 10.2 cm) and fuse one to the wrong side of each fat quarter.

2. Trace the Triangle template onto the fused fabric and cut out the triangle.

3. Arrange the triangles along the side of the skirt. Start with the turquoise triangle, and end with the red triangle.

4. Iron the triangles in place. If the length of the skirt varies, you may need to add another triangle or arrange the triangles so that the first one starts a bit higher or lower.

5. Zigzag-stitch around the triangles, changing the top thread to match each triangle.

MATERIALS

- 1 fat quarter
- Basic Sewing Kit (page 2)
- Ruler
- Long-sleeve T-shirt
- Matching thread

RUFFLE-EMBELLISHED SWEATER

Give a tee or an old cardigan new life with a sweet ruched neckline. Or try the same technique along the bottom edge of a flirty skirt.

DESIGN BY BEKI LAMBERT

1 FAT Quarter

INSTRUCTIONS

1. Cut the fat quarter into 2-inch (5.1 cm) strips.

2. Cut the T-shirt along the center front, turning it into a cardigan.

3. Place a strip of fabric, wrong side up, along the wrong side of one cut edge of the T-shirt (i.e., on the inside). Line up the edges. Pin in place. Trim the strip to match the length at the top and bottom edge. Sew the strip of fabric to the shirt along the edge using a ⅜-inch (9.5 mm) seam allowance.

4. At your ironing board, lay the edge of the T-shirt right side up and open the sewn strip flat—the sewn strip of fabric is wrong side up. Press the unsewn edge of the fabric strip ¼ inch (6 mm) to the wrong side. Fold the entire strip to the right side of the shirt. Enclose the raw edges of the shirt and the strip. Pin. Sew it in place along the folded outer edge. Zigzag along the top and bottom of the strip.

Repeat the process for the other side of the T-shirt.

5. Prepare the remaining strips of fabric into bobble trim: Fold the strip lengthwise into small accordion folds. Sew the folds in place every 2 inches (5.1 cm), by hand or with your sewing machine. Leave the last few inches unsewn on one end in case you need to sew it to another strip for more length.

6. Beginning at the neckline's open edge, tack one end of bobble trim to the neck. Use a needle and thread. Loop around the gathered part of the trim three or four times to secure it. Knot and cut the thread when done. Continue tacking the trim around the neckline until you reach the other end. Manipulate the bobbles so that you end on a gather.

7. Attach the bobble trim using the same process along the edges of the sewn fabric strips down the front of the T-shirt. At the neckline, tack the first gather of the trim under a neckline bobble. Add two more rows of bobble trim around the neck. Tack the beginning and ending gathers under a side bobble.

FINISHED SIZE

- 1⅛ inches (2.9 cm) each

MATERIALS

- 1 fat quarter with a small print and a variety of motifs
- Basic Sewing Kit (page 2)
- 3 half-ball cover button kits, 1⅛ inches (2.9 cm) each
- 1 transparency sheet
- Black permanent marker
- Scrap of white cotton fabric
- Fabric glue stick
- Perle cotton floss in to match the fat quarter

EMBROIDERED BUTTON COVERS

Wear your favorite fat quarter as a row of sweet, neat buttons. Great on a homemade sweater or an upcycled blazer, these buttons are hand-sewn and stylish.

DESIGN BY CYNTHIA SHAFFER

1 FAT Quarter

INSTRUCTIONS

1. Trace the button cover template that is provided on the back of the button package onto the transparency, using the black permanent marker, and then cut out.

2. Center a button top from the kit on the transparency circle from step 1, then trace around the button with the permanent marker.

3. Place the transparency circle on the fat-quarter fabric and search for fun motifs and designs. Use the inner marker circle as a guide to find those shapes and designs that will be embroidered.

4. Trace around the circle and cut out the fabric.

5. Place a button top on the white fabric and trace around the button, then cut out.

6. Glue the little white circle to the wrong side of the fabric circle. The white circle of fabric helps to reinforce the area of the button that will be embroidered.

7. Place a button top onto the right side of the fabric circle and trace around it with a water-soluble marker.

8. Embroider inside the marker circle. Fill in areas with French knots (page 5) and outline shapes with a

backstitch (page 5). Fill in the background with small random stitches.

9. Repeat steps 3 through 8 for the remaining two buttons.

PATCHWORK TIE

Turn your favorite fat quarter into a tie for dad or a dress-up accessory. With a wee patchwork strip insert, this project is clearly handmade and quite sophisticated.

DESIGN BY RUTH SINGER

1 FAT Quarter

FINISHED SIZE
• **4 x 54 inches (10.2 x 137.2 cm)**

MATERIALS
• **1 fat quarter for main fabric**
• **Basic Sewing Kit (page 2)**
• **Templates (pages 160–161)**
• **Long ruler**
• **Rotary cutter and mat (optional)**
• **4 or 5 charm squares or scraps for patchwork detail**
• **Cotton flannel or thick, soft sew-in interlining, 18 x 21 inches (45.7 x 53.3 cm)**
• **Lightweight fabric for lining, 6 inches square (15.2 cm)**
• **NOTE:** *The fabrics should be small-scale prints or semisolids that work well together.*

INSTRUCTIONS

1. Using the templates, cut the fat quarter into pieces (see Figure 1). Follow the straight grain marks carefully. Mark the balance points on each piece (in the seam allowances) to aid assembly.

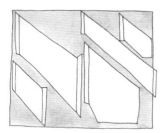

Figure 1

2. Cut a selection of charm squares or fabric scraps into six 1¼ x 2½-inch (3.2 x 6.4 cm) rectangles. The center rectangles will show, so choose your favorites to go in the middle of the strip. Join the rectangles along the narrow sides using ¼-inch (6 mm) seam allowances to make a strip with a total length of 12 inches (30.5 cm). Press seam allowances open. Mark the center line.

3. Join the patchwork strip to Piece A, right sides together, matching the balance marks. Each end will overlap by about ¼ inch (6 mm). Stitch with ¼-inch (6 mm) seam allowance. Press seam allowance toward Piece A.

4. Join the wider edge of Piece B to the patchwork strip, matching balance marks. Sew with ¼-inch (6 mm) seam allowance. Press seam allowance open and trim off excess at the side.

5. Continue building up the pieces, joining Pieces C and D and so on, always matching the longer end of each piece to the partial tie-front panel. Finish with Piece E. Trim all seam allowances and press seam allowances open.

6. Using the templates, cut the interlining piece and attach the two sections.

7. Using the templates, cut lining pieces from the lining fabric.

8. Place the tie and bigger piece of lining right sides together, matching points. Sew with ½-inch (1.3 cm) seam allowance, pivoting on the corner. Trim the tip.

9. Turn right side out and push the point out with a turning tool. Repeat on the narrow end with the other piece of lining. Press flat so the lining doesn't show on the front side.

10. With the tie-front fabric facedown, place the interlining inside the tie, tucking the points into place inside the lining pockets (see Figure 2). Press one long edge of the tie fabric under ³/₈ inch (9.5 mm).

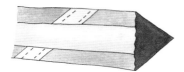

Figure 2

11. Fold over both sides of the tie along the edge of the interlining; the folded edge should lie on top. Hand-sew along the fold, catching both layers of tie fabric and the interlining.

GIVE & USE

FINISHED SIZE
- Each pop = 2⅛ x 3⅝ inches (5.4 x 9.21 cm)
- Tea towel = 19 square inches (48.26 cm)

MATERIALS
- 7 scraps of different fat quarter fabrics for the fruit pops and sticks
- Basic Sewing Kit (page 2)
- Templates (page 163)
- Fusible web
- 1 tea towel
- Ruler (optional)
- Coordinating threads

FRUIT POP TEA TOWEL

Oh, pile of rainbow scraps, you've found your calling! As a simple sewn gift or something special for your home, this tea towel is as cheery as it is handy.

DESIGN BY JENNIFER DAVIS

7 FAT Quarters

INSTRUCTIONS

1. Trace six Fruit Pop and Stick templates on fusible web. Cut around each shape, leaving a ¼-inch (6 mm) border, which helps the fusible web adhere better to the fabric.

NOTE: If you like, cut a "bite" out of one or more of your fruit pops.

2. Place the cutouts, sticky side down, on the wrong side of the fabric scraps. Attach them according to manufacturer's instructions. After the fabrics have cooled, cut them out on the drawn line.

3. Lay out your tea towel and arrange the fruit pops as desired: use a ruler to make sure everything is nice and

even. It helps to remove the backing from the shapes before you arrange them.

4. After you are satisfied with placement, carefully remove the fruit pops (leaving the sticks on the towel), and fuse the sticks to the towel. Then stitch them in place about ¹⁄₁₆ inch (1.6 mm) from the edge of the fabric using coordinating thread.

5. Next, arrange the fruit pops on top. When they are in place, fuse them to the tea towel according to manufacturer's instructions. Stitch down as before, using coordinating thread for each one.

PATCHWORK SEWING MACHINE COVER

Stow your beloved sewing machine in style. The clever piecing imitates special stitches (namely, cross, running, and zigzag), perfect for showcasing a few favorite fat quarters.

DESIGN BY AMY FRIEND

6 FAT Quarters

FINISHED SIZE
• 18 x 30 inches (45.7 x 76.2 cm)

MATERIALS
• 6 fat quarters in a variety of prints: 1 each of fabrics A, B, C, D, E, and F
• ½ yard (45.7 cm) of off-white fabric for the main fabric
• Basic Sewing Kit (page 2)
• Template (page 163)
• 22 x 34 inches (55.9 x 86.4 cm) batting and backing material
• **NOTE:** *All seam allowances are ¼ inch (6 mm) unless otherwise indicated.*

INSTRUCTIONS

1. From fabric A, cut 16 strips that are 4 x 2½ inches (10.2 x 6.4 cm). From the off-white background fabric, cut sixteen 2-inch (5.1 cm) squares and then cut the squares in half diagonally (creating half-square triangle units). Using these pieces and the paper-piecing template (page 162), paper-piece 16 small blocks to make the row of cross-stitches.

2. Once your blocks are trimmed, lay them out to form four Xs. First sew the top pieces of the X together and then the bottom pieces (see Figure 1). Press the seams in different directions so that they nest, and then stitch the tops and bottoms together.

Figure 1

3. Lay the finished blocks out to create a row of Xs and stitch them together. Remove the papers.

4. Set this aside and work on the row of straight stitches. Cut several 1½ x 2½-inch (3.8 x 6.4 cm) strips from fabric B and the off-white background fabric. Stitch the strips together on the short ends, alternating off-white and print pieces. Then add a 1½-inch (3.8 cm) off-white strip to the top and bottom.

5. With fabric C and off-white fabric, create the zigzag stitches using half-square triangle units that trim down to 2½ inches (6.4 cm) using whatever method you prefer (pages 6–7). You will need 16 units to create the zigzag. First stitch the top row together and then the bottom row, ironing the seams in different directions, then sew the strips together (see Figure 2).

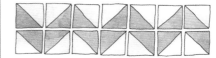

Figure 2

6. Assemble the rows of stitches. Center the row of straight stitches below the cross-stitches and then trim the edges flush. Add 1½-inch(3.8 cm) of off-white borders between the rows and along all four outer edges.

7. Next, trim down fabric D so it measures 18½ inches (47 cm) in one direction. Leave the width of the fat quarter as is and stitch the 18½-inch (47 cm) end to the upper edge of your finished panel. This is the completed exterior of your sewing machine cover. With the batting and the backing fabric, make your quilt sandwich and quilt as desired.

NOTE: For this sample, the designer used rows of closely spaced straight stitching.

8. To create the four ties for your cover, cut four strips of fabric E, each 2½ inches (6.4 cm) wide. Crease each lengthwise down the middle and press. Fold the outer edges into the center crease and press. Fold in half lengthwise and press again. Stitch along both the folded edge and the outer edge. Cut one end at an angle, measure 20 inches (51 cm) from the tip of the angle and cut straight. Tie a knot at each angled end.

9. Cut fabric F into strips that are 2½ inches (6.4 cm) wide for binding (pages 9–10). Stitch the binding to the outer edge of your cover, inserting the ties 7 inches (17.8 cm) up from the bottom edge on the front and back. Machine- or hand-sew the binding on the back and your cover is complete.

FINISHED SIZES

- Small: 5½-inch (14 cm) diameter, to fit a bowl up to 4 inches (10.2 cm)
- Medium: 10¼-inch (26 cm) diameter, to fit a bowl up to 8 inches (20.3 cm)
- Large: 14¾-inch (37.5 cm) diameter, to fit a bowl up to 13½ inches (34.3 cm)

MATERIALS

- 3 fat quarters: 1 of fabric A for either a small or medium cover, 2 of fabric B for a large cover
- Basic Sewing Kit (page 2)
- Templates (page 164)
- 50 inches (1.3 m) of elastic, ¼ inch (6 mm) wide
- Matching thread
- Safety pin

REUSABLE BOWL COVERS

Beautiful and brilliant, these lovelies can be used again and again. You'll love having them in your kitchen or make a set for a baker friend! Created with one fat quarter (or two for the large size), throw them in the wash when they're dirty.

DESIGN BY JESSICA FEDIW

3 FAT Quarters

NOTE: To cut two pieces for the medium-size bowl from one fat quarter, place the template at the far bottom right for the first cut and as far on the top left as possible for the second.

INSTRUCTIONS

1. Cut two circles of fabric from each template.

2. Cut three pieces of elastic: 10 inches (25.4 cm) for the small cover, 15 inches (38.1 cm) for the medium cover, 24 inches (61 cm) for the large cover.

3. For each cover, place one circle down, right side facing up. Place the second circle on top of it, matching the edges, wrong side facing up. Pin in place.

4. Sew together around the edges with a ¼-inch (6 mm) seam allowance, leaving a 3-inch (7.6 cm) opening for turning.

5. Turn right side out and press.

6. Sew around again, but this time 1 inch (2.5 cm) from the edges to create a casing for the elastic.

7. Place the safety pin on one end of each piece of elastic. Thread the pinned elastic through the opening and all the way around through the casing.

8. Sew the elastic ends together and push them into the fabric casing.

9. Turn in the raw edges of the fabric openings. Sew very close to the edge around the whole circle to sew the opening shut.

TIP: The fabric will need to be straightened at this point due to the elastic gathering it up.

FQ FLOWER TRIO

Perfect as brooches, hair clips, or as decorations, these fat quarter flowers are cheery, bright, and very easy to make.

DESIGN BY JESSICA FEDIW

5 FAT Quarters

POINTED PETALS BUTTON FLOWER

FINISHED SIZE
- 6-inch circle (15.2 cm)

MATERIALS
- 1 fat quarter
- Basic Sewing Kit (page 2)
- Template (page 165)
- Thread
- 1 button to coordinate with fabric, at least 1 inch (2.5 cm) in diameter

INSTRUCTIONS

1. Cut six 5-inch (12.7 cm) squares from the fat quarter.

2. Fold each square in half. Then fold in half the other way. There will be two folds.

3. Place the Pointed Petals template on the folds as indicated and cut out the flower. Repeat for each folded square.

4. Keeping them folded, hand-sew the six pieces together at the corners of the folds. Alternate where the edges face so they spread out to make a full flower.

5. Hand-sew a button in the middle.

POM-POM FLOWER

FINISHED SIZE

- 4 x 4 x 2½ inches (10.2 x 10.2 x 6.4 cm)

MATERIALS

- 1 fat quarter
- Scissors
- Ruler or tape measure
- 1 scrap of fabric for tying the center
- Hot-glue gun and glue stick

INSTRUCTIONS

1. Starting at a corner of the fat quarter, begin cutting 1 inch (2.5 cm) from edge. Continue cutting straight until 1 inch (2.5 cm) from the opposite edge. Then turn your cutting to continue going around the whole fat quarter until you are 1 inch (2.5 cm) from the beginning cut. Keep cutting around the whole fat quarter 1 inch (2.5 cm) from the edges until you reach the center. You will have one long piece of 1-inch-wide (2.5 cm) fabric.

2. Trim and round the corner edges.

3. Wrap the fabric loosely around your hand, then remove it while keeping it all together. Tie it in the middle with a piece of scrap fabric.

4. Trim the fabric loops on each side until there are no more fabric folds and it looks like a puffy ball. You want the fabric lengths to all be about the same length to achieve this look.

5. Hot-glue the "petals" together at the middle to help the flower look fuller and to hide the scrap-fabric tie.

3-LAYERED SCALLOPED EDGE FLOWER

FINISHED SIZE

- 4½ inches square (11.4 cm)

MATERIALS

- 3 fat quarters
- Templates (page 165)
- 3 fat quarters
- Scissors
- 1 piece of scrap fabric for middle of petals
- Hand-sewing needle
- Thread

INSTRUCTIONS

1. Using the Scalloped Edge templates, cut out the three flower petals using one different fat quarter fabric for each size.

2. Cut out the Middle section from scrap fabric. Snip straight down many times all along the top width to create a fringe. Baste along the bottom edge and gather. Sew ends together.

3. Stack the three petals on top of each other, right sides facing up and matching the centers. Place the Middle section in the center, fringe facing up, and bring the flower petals up around it. Sew them all together at the center bottom.

CATHEDRAL WINDOW PINCUSHION

Part origami project, part fabric puzzle, this pincushion is delightful to make, and fun to look at and use in your sewing space.

DESIGN BY HEATHER FRENCH

3
FAT
Quarters

FINISHED SIZE
• **4 inches square (10.2 cm)**

MATERIALS
• **3 assorted fat quarters**
• **Basic Sewing Kit (page 2)**
• **Rotary cutter and mat**
• **Gridded ruler**
• **4 pieces of solid-color fabric for the corners, each 2 inches square (5.1 cm)**
• **4 small buttons**
• **Polyester fiberfill**

INSTRUCTIONS

1. Using the rotary cutter, mat, and gridded ruler, cut the following from the fat quarters:

- Two 10-inch (25.4 cm) squares of edging and contrasting fabric (from solid and white print fat quarters for this sample).
- One 6½-inch (16.5 cm) square of background fabric (from red print fat quarter for this sample).
- One 5½-inch (14 cm) square of bottom fabric.

2. Make the first layer by sewing the two 10-inch (25.4 cm) squares together with right sides facing, leaving a gap for turning. Turn right side out and press. Hand-stitch the gap closed.

3. Find the center point of this square and press each corner in on itself to meet the center point (the patterned fabric is inside).

4. Press each of these corners back on itself by 1 inch (2.5 cm) (see Figure 1).

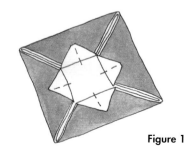

Figure 1

5. Unfold the corners and position the 6½-inch (16.5 cm) square of background fabric in the center (see Figure 2).

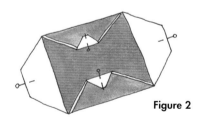

Figure 2

6. Refold all corners and pin through all layers.

7. Make the second layer by folding the outer corners in 2 inches (5.1 cm) and pressing.

8. Position a 2-inch (5.1 cm) solid square underneath each 1-inch (2.5 cm) folded corner and pin (see Figure 3). Refold all corners (see Figure 4). Your piece should now measure 5 inches square (12.5 cm).

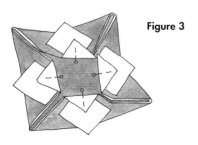

Figure 3

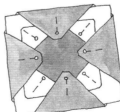

Figure 4

9. Pin each side of the outer triangles and sew along each edge to create the cathedral window effect.

10. Attach buttons to the point of each triangle.

11. Place the square of bottom fabric that measures 5½-inches (14 cm) on the pieced square, right sides together. Using a ½-inch (1.3 cm) seam allowance, sew around all sides, leaving a 2-inch (5.1 cm) gap for turning.

12. Trim the corners and seam allowance and turn right side out.

13. Press, stuff with fiberfill, and hand-stitch the gap closed.

FINISHED SIZE

- 8 inch circle (20.3 cm)

MATERIALS

- 2 fat quarters: 1 of fabric A for the main potholder, 1 of fabric B for the binding
- Basic Sewing Kit (page 2)
- Circular template, 8 inches (20.3 cm) in diameter
- Insulated quilt batting, 17 x 25 inches (43.2 x 63.5 cm)
- Ruler
- Coordinating thread
- Bias tape maker (optional)
- NOTE: *An 8-inch (20.3 cm) dessert plate works great as a template for the potholder.*

CIRCLE HOT POT PADS

Perk up your kitchen with this simple, sweet, and useful set of potholders that can double up as a trivet for hot dishes on your table. To make them, all you need is a coordinating pair of fat quarters.

DESIGN BY JENNY BARTOY

INSTRUCTIONS

1. Cut the following pieces:

   - Using the template, trace and cut four circles from fabric A.

   - Four strips from fabric B, each 2 x 18 inches (5.1 x 45.7 cm).

   - Using the template, trace and cut four circles from the quilt batting. These are the inside layers for the potholders—two each.

2. Create a potholder sandwich with the cut circles: one layer of fabric A, right side down; two layers of insulated batting; one layer of fabric A, right side up. Repeat for the second potholder. Press and pin all these layers securely together.

NOTE: Follow the manufacturer's instructions for working with insulated batting.

3. With a ruler and a fabric marker, draw a grid on the top fabric. Follow this grid to quilt the potholder. You can space lines 1 to 1½ inches (2.5 to 3.8 cm) apart.

4. Quilt your potholders by stitching along the grid lines with coordinating thread. Start in the middle, creating a large X, then make your way toward the edges with every line of stitches. Remove pins as you go. Trim any excess fabric and batting around your 8-inch (20.3 cm) circle potholders.

5. Create your binding tape (see page 10). Line up two fabric B strips at the short end, right sides together. Pin and sew them together, ¼ inch (6 mm) from the edge. Press the seam open. Repeat with the remaining two strips.

6. You should have two 35-inch (88.9 cm) strips. Pressing with a full steam iron, run these strips through a bias tape maker or fold ½ inch (1.3 cm) in along each long edge length to create single-fold 1-inch (2.5 cm) binding tape.

7. Bind the first potholder (pages 9–10). Leaving a 6-inch (15.2 cm) tail, begin pinning the bias tape around

the potholder, with right sides together and matching edges. Sew the binding onto the potholder with a ½-inch (1.3 cm) allowance, stitching the bias tails together before you get back to your starting place.

8. Fold the binding tape over the edge of the potholder and press, making sure it covers the stitches you just made all around the edge. Pin it in place.

9. Front side up, stitch in the ditch (in the seam between the potholder fabric and binding, see page 10) all the way around the potholder. This should catch the binding on the back and properly finish your potholder.

10. Repeat steps 7 through 9 with the second quilted sandwich and strips. Your potholders or trivets are now ready to use.

KEY FOB

You'll never lose your keys again if they're attached to your favorite fabric! These lovelies make great party favors and teacher's gifts that will be appreciated for their charm— and you will be appreciated for your thoughtfulness.

DESIGN BY MEGAN HUNT

1-2
FAT
Quarters

FINISHED SIZE

- **1 x 6 inches (2.5 x 15.2 cm)**

MATERIALS

- **1 or 2 fat quarters**
- **Basic Sewing Kit (page 2)**
- **Fray retardant**
- **1 key-fob hardware with split ring for each fob, 1 inch (2.5 cm)**
- **Pliers**

INSTRUCTIONS

1. Cut two 2 x 11-inch (5.1 x 27.9 cm) strips from your fabric.

2. Fold in the raw edges of each fabric strip ½ inch (1.3 cm) and press into place with a hot iron.

3. Put the two strips on top of each other, wrong sides together.

4. Topstitch along the edges of the two layers to sew them together, staying as close to the edge as you can.

5. Trim the ends of the fabric strip and seal the ends with fray retardant.

6. Fold the strip in half with the main fabric right side out, and make sure the ends are flush with one another.

7. Center the fabric strip inside the key fob hardware and use pliers to close the grips around the fabric.

FINISHED SIZE

- **Small book cover:** 9¼ x 6¼ inches (23.5 x 15.9 cm), flap: 1⁷/₁₆ x 6¼ inches (3.7 x 15.9 cm)
- **Medium book cover:** 11⁷/₈ x 8⁵/₈ inches (30.2 x 21.9 cm), flap: 2 x 8⁵/₈ inches (5.1 x 21.9 cm)
- **Large book cover:** 12½ x 8⁵/₈ inches (31.8 x 21.9 cm), flap: 1¹³/₁₆ x 8⁵/₈ inches (4.6 x 21.9 cm)
- **Bookmarks:** 5 x 1¾ inches (12.7 x 4.4 cm)

MATERIALS (TO MAKE ONE)

- 1 fat quarter (see note below)
- Basic Sewing Kit (page 2)
- Notebook
- Embroidery floss for the cover (optional) plus floss to match the fabric
- 4½ inches (11.4 cm) of ribbon, ½ inch (1.3 cm) wide
- Matching thread
- Template (page 164)
- **NOTE:** *As long as your book is 6 x 8 inches (15.2 x 20.3 cm) or smaller, all parts of the cover will fit on one fat quarter. If it is larger than this, you will need two fat quarters.*

BOOK COVER WITH BOOKMARK

Jot special notes or sketch design ideas in a handy fat-quarter-encased notebook. Made with a single fat quarter (or more, for larger sketchbooks), these journals whip up quickly and make great gifts.

DESIGN BY CARINA ENVOLDSEN-HARRIS

1-2 FAT Quarters

INSTRUCTIONS

1. Calculate the width of the cover by measuring the whole width of the book, from the side edge of the front to the side edge of the back, including the spine, and add ½ inch (1.3 cm) to this measurement. It is important that the book is closed when you measure it. If it is laid open, the cover will not fit.

2. Calculate the height of the cover by measuring the height of the book and add ¾ inch (1.9 cm).

3. Calculate the flaps by measuring two-thirds of the front cover only and add ½ inch (1.3 cm). Use your calculation from step 2 for the height of the flaps.

4. Cut two cover pieces and two flap pieces using these measurements from the fat quarter or fat quarters.

5. If you want to add embroidery to your cover, stitch it on the right-hand side of the outside cover, leaving at least a

1-inch (2.5 cm) margin at the outer edges and the middle.

6. Fold the flap pieces in half lengthwise with right sides facing out.

7. Place the two cover pieces together with right sides facing.

8. Place one folded flap piece at each end and with the raw edges together, between the two cover layers. The folded edge of the flaps should point toward the middle of the covers.

9. Mark the middle of the front cover's top edge, then mark 1 inch (2.5 cm) to the right of that.

10. Cut two bookmark pieces using the Bookmark template from the fat quarter fabric. If the fabric is patterned, remember to reverse one piece.

11. Pin the two pieces together with wrong sides facing each other. Pin the ribbon in place along the straight edge of the bookmark pieces.

12. Hand-stitch the bookmark pieces together using a blanket stitch (page 5).

13. Pin the bookmark ribbon, tucked between the cover layers, in place at the 1-inch (2.5 cm) mark on the front cover.

14. Along the bottom edge of the cover, mark 2 inches (5.1 cm) on both sides of the middle. This will be the turning gap.

15. Sew all the way around the cover with a ¼-inch (6 mm) seam allowance. Leave the turning gap open.

16. Clip the corners and turn the cover right side out. Push the corners out so they are nice and sharp. Use a turning tool or the eraser end of a pencil if necessary.

17. Using matching thread and a ⅛-inch (3 mm) seam allowance, topstitch over the turning gap to close it.

18. Press all the seams and insert the notebook.

SAMPLE BOOK DIMENSIONS

These are the measurements needed for a 5½ x 8-inch (14 x 20.3 cm) book with a ½-inch (1.3 cm) spine.

- Cover width: 5½ (front) + 5½ (back) + ½ (spine) + ½ inch (14 + 14 + 1.3 +1.3 cm) = 12 inches (30.5 cm)
- Cover height: 8 + ¾ inch (20.3 + 1.9 cm) = 8¾ inches (22.2 cm)
- Each flap: (5½ x ⅔) + ½ inches ([14 x 1.7] + 1.3 cm) = 4⅙ inches (10.6 cm) wide; 8 + ¾ inches (20.3 x 1.9 cm) = 8 ¾ inches (22.2 cm) high

If the cover of your book is thicker than $\frac{1}{16}$ inch (1.6 mm), include this in your measurement calculations (remember to double it for two covers).

FINISHED SIZE

• **4¾ x 4 x 4 inches (12 x 10.2 x 10.2 cm)**

MATERIALS

• **27 pieces of assorted fat quarter fabrics for the outer basket patchwork, 2½ inches square (6.4 cm)**
• **Basic Sewing Kit (page 2)**
• **Coordinating thread**
• **Batting, 8 x 20 inches (20.3 x 50.8 cm)**
• **Basting pins or spray**
• **Ruler**
• **Rotary cutter and mat**
• **1 piece of fabric B for inner basket lining, 6 x 18 inches (15.2 x 45.7 cm)**
• **1 piece of fabric C for inner pocket, 6 inches square (15.2 cm)**
• **1 piece of fabric D for basket loop, 2 x 6 inches (5.1 x 15.2 cm)**

SEWING CADDY

Made with simple piecing and boxed corners, this sewing caddy provides a clever catchall for snipped threads, embroidery scissors, and other tiny tools that need storing.

DESIGN BY MAUREEN CRACKNELL

27 FAT Quarters

INSTRUCTIONS

1. Lay out the fabric squares into three rows of nine. Using a ¼-inch (6 mm) seam allowance, sew 9 squares together for each row. Sew the rows together.

2. Lay the sewn patchwork front, right side up, onto the piece of batting. Baste in place, using pins or basting spray.

3. Add straight quilting stitches ¼ inch (6 mm) from each seam going across and down the patchwork.

4. When finished, use a ruler, mat, and rotary cutter to trim the patchwork front to measure 6 x 18 inches (15.2 x 45.7 cm).

5. Fold the quilted patchwork basket front piece in half crosswise, right sides together, so that it measures 6 x 9 inches (15.2 x 22.9 cm) and pin along the open side and bottom edges.

6. Sew the open side and bottom edges using a ¼-inch (6 mm) seam allowance.

7. Create boxed corners (page 6) to form the basket sides and bottom. First form a triangle at the corner edge.

8. Mark a sewing line 2 inches (5.1 cm) from the corner point.

9. With a pen or marker, draw on that line, pin, and sew down it with a straight stitch.

10. Trim the corner ¼ inch (6 mm) from the outer edge of that seam. Repeat steps 7 through 9 for the other side.

11. Fold the pocket fabric C in half to measure 3 x 6 inches (7.6 x 15.2 cm).

12. Sew a ¼-inch (6 mm) seam around two sides of the pocket, leaving one short end open. Carefully trim away the corner edges.

13. Turn the fabric C pocket right side out and fold in the open edge ¼ inch (6 mm); press with iron to set.

14. Measuring 2 inches (5.1 cm) from the side of fabric B and 1 inch (2.5 cm) from the top, pin the fabric C pocket in place along each side and the bottom.

15. Attach the pocket by sewing close to the outer edge along both sides and the bottom, removing the pins as you go.

16. With chalk or a sewing pin, mark a line down the center of the pocket and sew on that line to create two pocket openings.

17. Fold the fabric B lining piece in half so that it measures 6 x 9 inches (15.2 x 22.9 cm) and pin it closed along the open side and bottom edges.

18. Sew the lining closed along the pinned side and bottom edges using a ¼-inch (6 mm) seam allowance.

19. Follow steps 7 through 10 to square off the corners and finish the lining.

20. Fold fabric D in half to measure 1 x 6 inches (2.5 x 15.2 cm).

21. Sew a scant ¼-inch (6 mm) seam along the long edge only to form a tube.

22. Use a turning tool to turn the loop right side out and press with an iron to set.

23. Fold to create the loop and attach the loop to the back center of the patchwork basket piece.

24. Place the outer patchwork basket piece inside the lining piece with right sides facing, matching up the open edges and side seams, and pin in place.

25. Sew ¼ inch (6 mm) from the edge, leaving an opening for turning the basket right side out.

26. Turn out the basket right side out, turn in the edges of the opening, and pin.

27. Topstitch around the top edge and close the opening.

TEMPLATES

CHILD'S FQ
REVERSIBLE APRON
(page 13)

copy at 166%

ARMHOLE PATTERN

Cut 2 from each fat quarter

Includes 3/8-inch (9.525 cm) seam
allowance on all sides

SWEET DREAMS
TODDLER SHEETS
(page 17)

STITCH PATTERN
copy at 143%

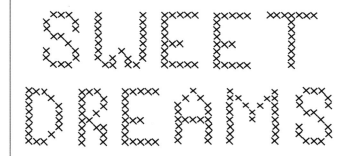

HEXAGONS
copy at 100%

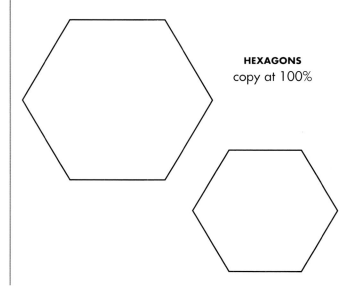

FAT QUARTER PARTY HATS
(page 21)

copy at 200%

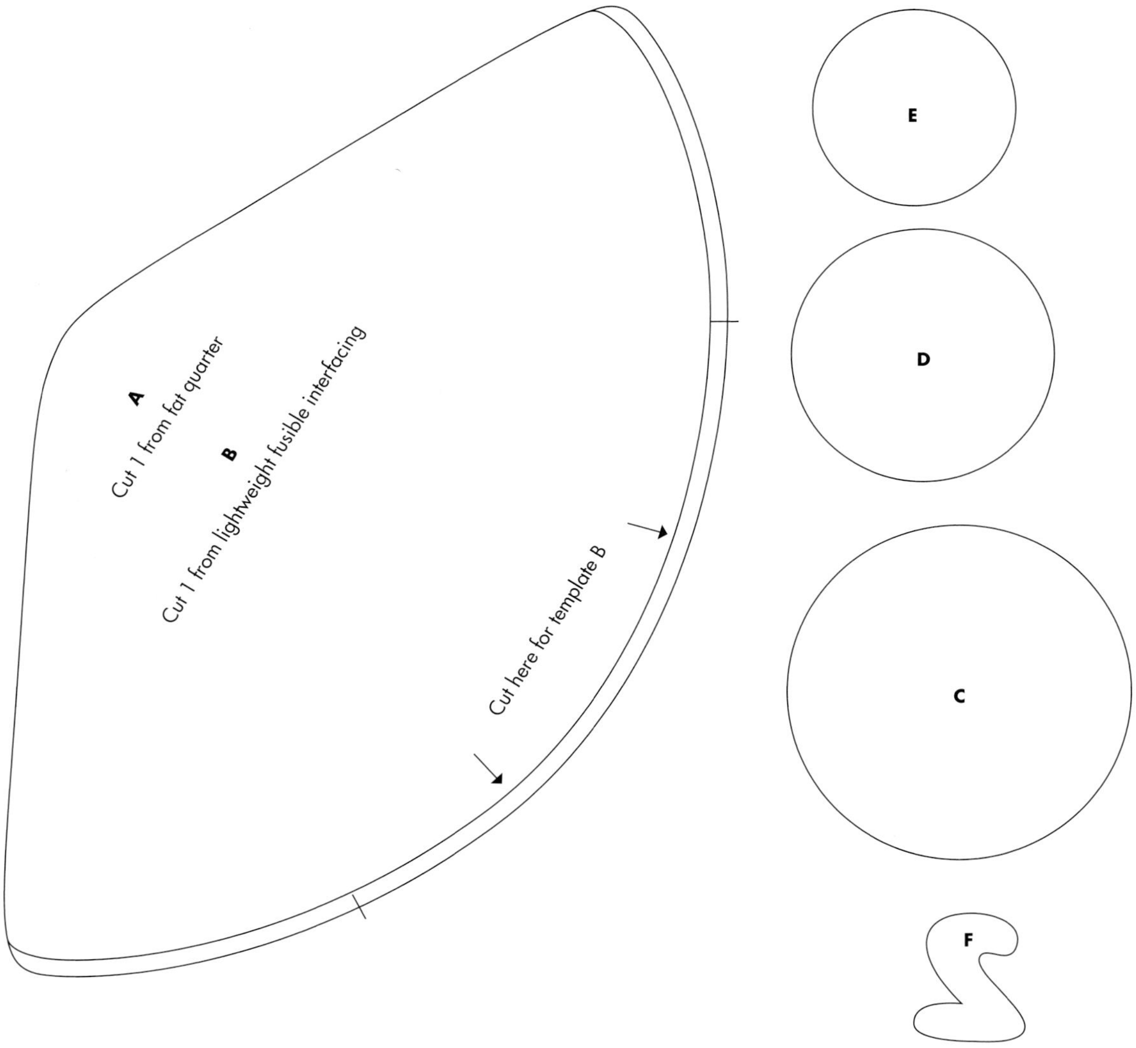

A

Cut 1 from fat quarter

B

Cut 1 from lightweight fusible interfacing

Cut here for template B

E

D

C

F

FQ BABY DRESS
(page 25)
copy at 294%

FRONT

Cut 1 on fold.

BACK

Cut 2.

TOY APPLE WITH WORM
(page 27)
copy at 200%

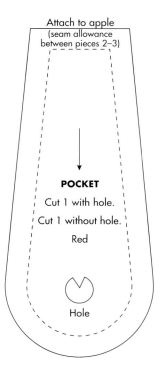

Attach to apple
(seam allowance
between pieces 2–3)

POCKET

Cut 1 with hole.

Cut 1 without hole.

Red

Hole

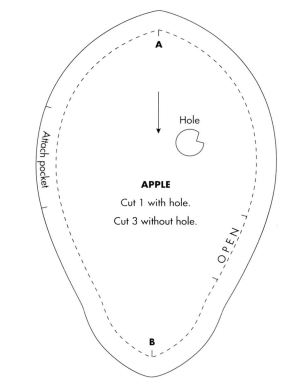

A

Hole

Attach pocket

APPLE

Cut 1 with hole.

Cut 3 without hole.

OPEN

B

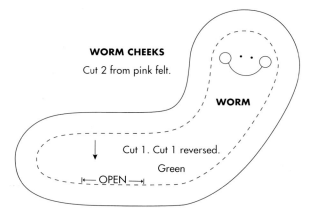

WORM CHEEKS

Cut 2 from pink felt.

WORM

Cut 1. Cut 1 reversed.

Green

OPEN

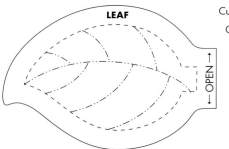

LEAF

Cut 1. Cut 1 reversed.

Cut 1 from batting.

OPEN

FLOPPY ANIMAL FRIENDS
(page 30)
copy at 133%

SOFT-SHAPED TOYS & POUCH
(page 33)
copy at 200%

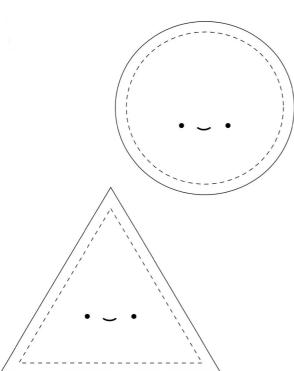

DIAPER HOLDER & BURP CLOTH
(page 35)
copy at 100%

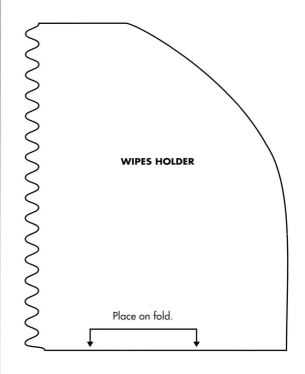

WIPES HOLDER

Place on fold.

MUSHROOM TOTE
(page 37)
copy at 222%

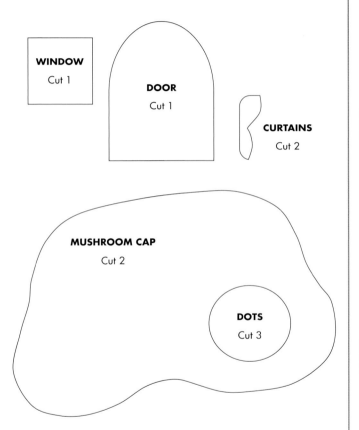

WINDOW
Cut 1

DOOR
Cut 1

CURTAINS
Cut 2

MUSHROOM CAP
Cut 2

DOTS
Cut 3

BABY FOOD JAR BIB
(page 41)
copy at 263%

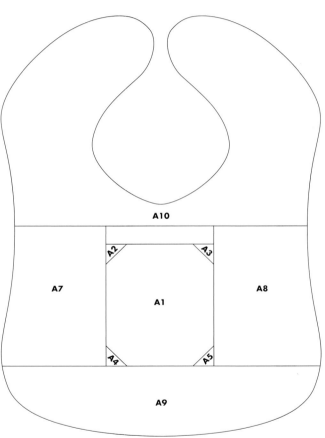

A10

A2

A3

A7

A1

A8

A4

A5

A9

CHILD'S TRAVEL PLACEMAT
(page 42)
copy at 166%

COOL TABLET CASE
(page 49)
copy at 125%

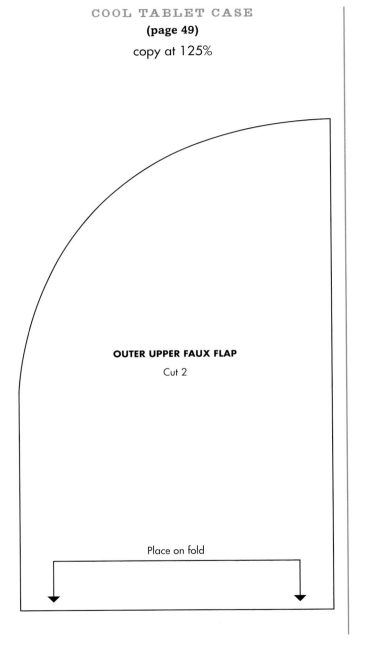

OUTER UPPER FAUX FLAP

Cut 2

Place on fold

LIBRARY TOTE
(page 55)
copy at 166%

BOOK MOTIFS

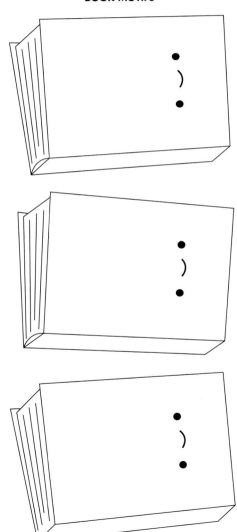

OVAL POCKET HANDBAG
(page 61)

copy at 181%

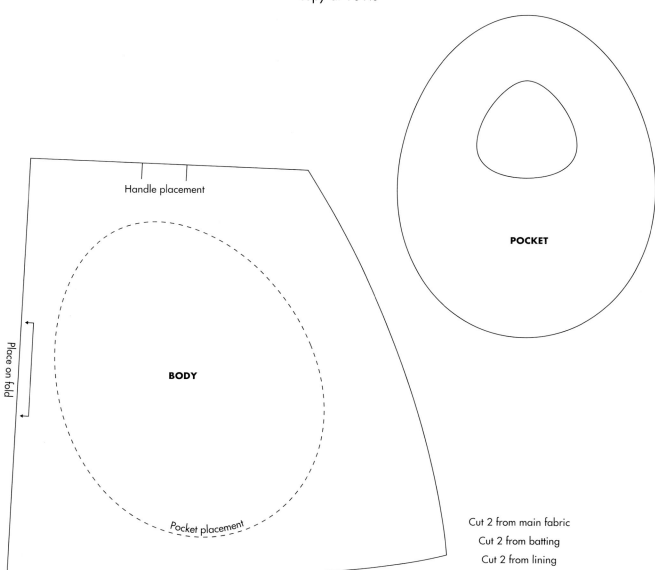

Handle placement

Place on fold

BODY

Pocket placement

POCKET

Cut 2 from main fabric

Cut 2 from batting

Cut 2 from lining

ARROWHEAD CLUTCH
(page 67)
copy at 100%

GROOVY VIBES QUILT
(page 75)
copy at 143%

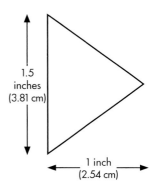

1.5
inches
(3.81 cm)

1 inch
(2.54 cm)

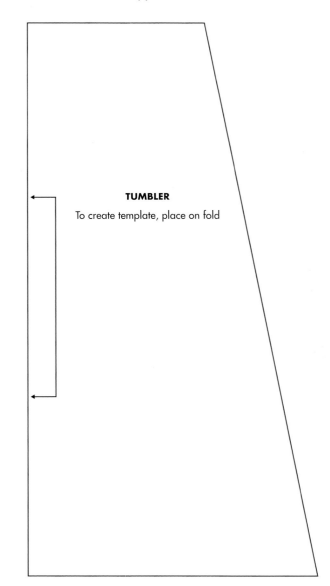

TUMBLER
To create template, place on fold

HOTHOUSE PILLOW SET
(page 76)
copy at 200%

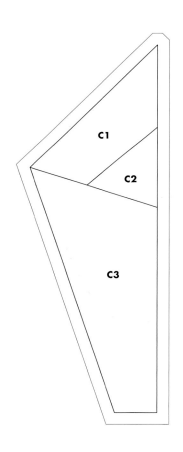

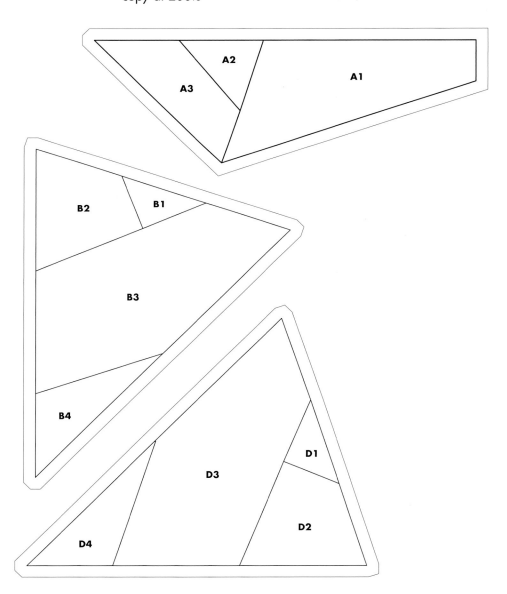

ALL MY HEART MINI QUILT
(page 85)
copy at 100%

HEART

HOOP TREE
(page 101)
copy at 100%

APPLE

RAINBOW CHEVRON SKIRT
(page 119)
copy at 100%

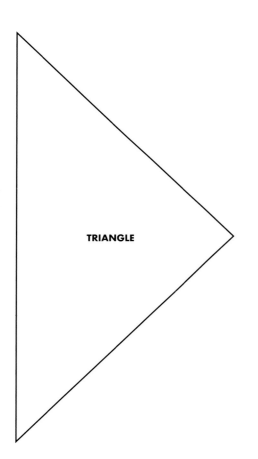

TRIANGLE

PATCHWORK TIE
(page 124)
copy at 476%

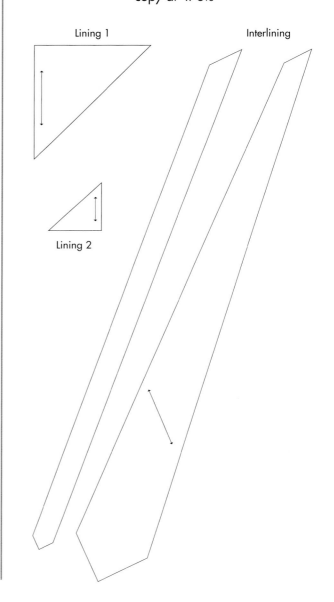

Lining 1

Interlining

Lining 2

copy at 400%

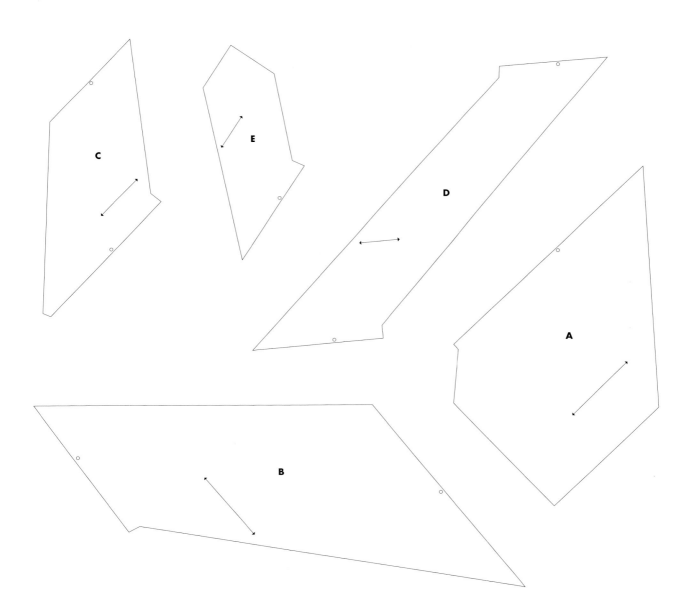

FABRIC BIRDS
(page 103)
copy at 250%

CHEERS COASTER SET
(page 109)
copy at 133%

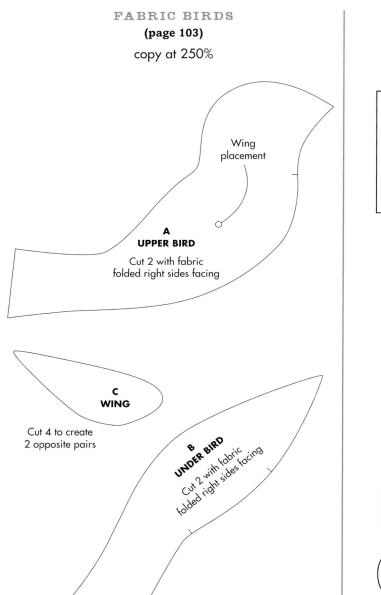

Wing placement

A
UPPER BIRD
Cut 2 with fabric
folded right sides facing

C
WING

Cut 4 to create
2 opposite pairs

B
UNDER BIRD
Cut 2 with fabric
folded right sides facing

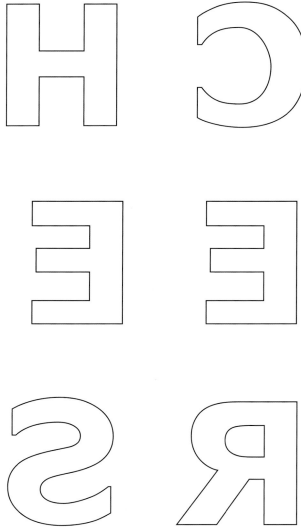

FRUIT POP TEA TOWELS
(page 127)
copy at 100%

FRUIT POP

STICK

PATCHWORK SEWING MACHINE COVER
(page 128)
copy at 100%

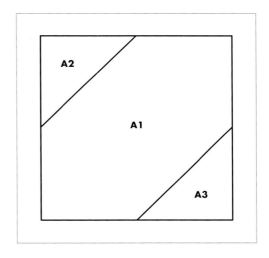

A2

A1

A3

REUSABLE BOWL COVERS
(page 131)
copy at 476%

BOOK COVER WITH BOOKMARK
(page 141)
copy at 100%

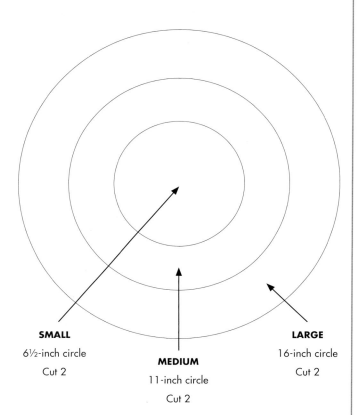

SMALL

6½-inch circle

Cut 2

MEDIUM

11-inch circle

Cut 2

LARGE

16-inch circle

Cut 2

BOOKMARK

NOTES

FQ FLOWER TRIO
(page 132)
copy at 166%

POINTED PETALS

Place on fold

Place on fold

SCALLOPED EDGE

Cut 6 from fabric

MIDDLE SECTION

ABOUT THE DESIGNERS

ANNELIESE

Anneliese is the mother of three daughters who keep her busy and ever inspired. She designs the children's sewing pattern line, Wee Muses, and she journals online about the celebrations of her life and of her pursuits to create beautiful things.
AestheticNest.com

JENNY BARTOY

Jenny creates upcycled fiber art and handmade textile goods for the home that she sells in her shop on Etsy. Inspired by nature, patchwork, and clean design, she loves to work with natural materials and modern fabrics. Jenny is a mama of two curious boys and a former project manager and filmmaker. She lives in beautiful Seattle, Washington with her archaeologist husband, their sons, and one rambunctious kitty.
www.jennybartoy.com

MARILYN BUTLER

Marilyn spends most of her weekdays with her two young grandchildren, basking in their natural enthusiasm and curiosity. Evenings and weekends are spent with her husband and other family members—and in her sewing room. Creating for as long as she can recall, a designated space for sewing and quilting is a luxury and a necessity. Playing with fabric, color, and design keeps her sometimes crazy life in balance. Marilyn also enjoys embroidery and English paper piecing. She is a member of the Kansas City Modern Quilt Guild and participates in a variety of online quilting groups.
marilynbutler.blogspot.com.

LINDSAY CONNER

Lindsay is the author of *Modern Bee: 13 Quilts to Make with Friends* and she's contributed sewing patterns to a number of books and magazines. A writer, editor, and quilter, she lives in Nashville, Tennessee with her husband, son, and two loveable cats, Murph and Chloe.
LindsaySews.com
CraftBuds.com

SHANNON COOK

Shannon is a knitting and sewing pattern designer, blogger, author, publisher, wife, and mom to two daughters. She is happily living a handmade life near the ocean on Vancouver Island, BC. Shannon designs patterns for the modern knitter and sewer. With their engaging textures, vibrant colors, and striking lines, her fun, dynamic garments and accessories are destined to become wardrobe staples. She's also the co-author and co-publisher of *SEASONLESS* (2014) and *JOURNEY* (2013).
www.veryshannon.com

MAUREEN CRACKNELL

Maureen is a lover of all things crafty & creative, and makes things by hand, at home in small town Pennsylvania. She started blogging in 2010 for a little space to share her passion to create, to document her learning and growth as an artistic person, and to have a special place to keep and share her projects and those special moments that she and her children create together throughout their days. Maureen feels so incredibly thankful to be a part of the online sewing community and so blessed to be able to make and seek out new artistic goals because of the support and encouragement she receives!
www.maureencracknellhandmade.blogspot.com

JENNIFER DAVIS

Jennifer is a military wife, mom, and teacher's assistant, living the good life in the great state of Wyoming. Her plethora of hobbies (sewing, cooking, knitting, crochet, cross-stitching, and reading, to name a few) keep her busy during the Wyoming winters. Likes: all things British, libraries, donuts, Coca-Cola, and Kawaii *anything*. Dislikes: bad grammar, sad endings, and pessimists. You can find her on Instagram as user "sugar_stitches."

MALKA DUBRAWSKY

Having first discovered the world of crafting in eighth-grade art class, Malka went on to earn a BFA in Studio Art. Her interest in textiles developed as a result of spending time at home with her children. Having spent several years primarily as a fiber artist, Malka Dubrawsky has turned to designing functional textiles as she continues to focus on using her own hand-dyed and patterned fabrics. This has led Malka to design quilts, pillows, and other items that can be found at her online store. Malka also writes and designs patterns, with her work appearing in a variety of magazines and books. She has authored *Color Your Cloth: A Quilter's Guide to Dying and Patterning Fabric* (Lark Books, 2009) and *Fresh Quilting: Fearless Color, Design and Inspiration* (2010).
stitchindye.blogspot.com.

CARINA ENVOLDSEN-HARRIS

Carina is an author, designer, and craft blogger. Originally from Denmark, she now lives outside London with her husband. Under the name Polka & Bloom, she designs colorful, free-form embroidery patterns and fabric designs. Carina is the author of *Stitched Blooms* (Lark, 2013).
carinascraftblog.com
shop.polkaandbloom.com

JESSICA FEDIW

Jessica is a wife and a mom to two beautiful little girls. Her husband is in the Coast Guard, so she gets to move around and see parts of the U.S. that she might not have otherwise. She loves crafting, with sewing and crocheting being her favorites. She began blogging about her creations when her oldest daughter was 1 and hasn't stopped since.
www.happytogetherbyjess.com

AMY FRIEND

Amy is a designer, quilter, and sewer who blogs at During Quiet Time. She has worked with BasicGrey to create quilt designs, with Art Gallery Fabrics as a member of their Fat Quarter Gang, as a project designer for Thermoweb, and design team member for Sizzix, and also sells her patterns on Etsy and Craftsy. Additionally, Amy's projects have appeared in *American Quilter, McCall's Quick Quilts*, and *Fat Quarterly Ezine*, as well as in several books.
duringquiettime.com

HEATHER JEAN FRENCH

Heather Jean is a freelance surface pattern designer specializing in textiles design. She works across a range of areas and has experience in fashion and interiors. Her work has a retro theme with a geometric twist and is all printed by hand.

She has worked in textiles for a number of years as a designer-maker and also teaches, delivering sewing workshops both for private clients and community organizations. Her lessons specialize in bag making but she also offers hand-sewn projects.

ABBY GLASSENBERG

Abby, who creates unique patterns for stuffed animals, has shared her creations and her ideas on design, technique, and the online culture of craft through her blog, While She Naps since 2005. Abby's latest book, *Stuffed Animals: From Concept to Construction* (Lark Crafts, 2013) was named an Amazon Best Book of the Year in 2013. Her first book, *The Artful Bird: Feathered Friends To Make and Sew* (2011), was an ALA Booklist top 10 craft book.

www.whileshenaps.com

VICTORIA GUTHRIE

Vick is a crafter and freelance writer. She has worked as editor of a quilting magazine and writes for a wide selection of craft magazines. She loves sewing, quilting, baking, and jewelery making. Vick lives in Suffolk, England with her partner and five cats, Peanut, Temperance, D'Artagnan, Gordon, and Hunter.

craftygoodness.co.uk

MEGAN HUNT

The author of *Fabric Blooms: 42 Flowers to Make, Wear, and Adorn Your Life* (Lark Crafts, 2014), Megan is also the voice behind the successful lifestyle and creative blog, Princess Lasertron. In addition, she is a wedding designer and creator of custom flower bouquets and dresses, which she sells through her Princess Lasertron shop. The Princess Lasertron brand has reached hundreds of thousands of brides and readers through magazines, television, and online media including: *Brides* magazine, *Cosmopolitan Bride*, *Country Living*, *Forbes*, and others. Megan recently cofounded Hello Holiday, an online fashion startup that offers support and funding to new designers. Because of her marketing intuition and ability to make emotional connections with a community of customers, Megan speaks at creative and entrepreneurial conferences around the country. She and her young daughter Alice live in Omaha, Nebraska.

princesslasertron.com

MOLLIE JOHANSON

Mollie, a trained graphic designer specializing in print projects, began her blog Wild Olive as an outlet for more whimsical works. Daily dreaming and doodling have resulted in a variety of embroidery and paper projects, most featuring simply expressive faces. Mollie, based in a far western suburb of Chicago, commutes daily to her in-home studio via the coffee pot.

wildolive.blogspot.com

TARA KOLESNIKOWICZ

With a two-year-old and an infant around, it was too easy for Tara to get lost in being a mom. Realizing she was missing the "creative" part of her life, she started her blog, SewTara. Journaling what she was creating was a promise to herself to create regularly. Soon there were comments, new friends, and great experiences. Eventually a shop on Etsy came about. Most of her items have some sort of environmental twist and either avoid sending more things to a landfill or use repurposing thrift finds, or every last possible usable scrap.

www.sewtara.com

BEKI LAMBERT

Beki loves collecting beautiful fabrics and using them to make bags, quilts, pillows, and dresses for her girls. She also designs fabulous tote bags and sells PDFs online that enable you to make them yourself. Schedule permitting, Beki may accept special orders. The mom of four young kids with a passion for making things in her spare time, Beki is sure her creative outlet is what keeps her sane. In addition to publishing and selling her own PDF sewing patterns, her designs have been included in several books, including the Pretty Little series by Lark Books and the *Craft Hope* book, also by Lark (2010). You can find out what's going on in Beki's artsy-crafty household, or see what projects she's currently working on by visiting her blog.

artsycraftybabe.com.

www.etsy.com/shop/artsycraftybabe

KAYE PRINCE

Kaye is a mild-mannered librarian by day but a sailor-mouthed pattern designer, and consummately crafty person, the rest of the time. She has a particular fondness for any craft that can incorporate patchwork, llamas, and baby polar bears (a girl can dream right?). She enjoys keeping up to date with her creations and sharing those things that make her smile on her blog.

kayeprince.com

JENNIFER RODRIGUEZ

Jennifer is a mother of three, wife, and artist in West Jordan, Utah. On most early mornings and late nights, she can be found creating textile art and mixed-media creations in her studio. Fueled by Diet Coke and her children's laughter, she is inspired daily to make something meaningful.

Her artwork has been featured in *Art Quilting Studio*, *Quilting Arts*, and *Stitch*. You can find quilting patterns designed by her on the Moda Bakeshop website as well as Riley Blake's Cutting Corners. From fabric to polymer clay, she is inspired by color and texture.

AllThingsBelle.blogspot.com

CYNTHIA SHAFFER

Cynthia is a quilter, creative sewer, and photographer whose love of fabric can be traced back to childhood. She learned to sew at age 6 and in no time was designing and sewing clothing for herself and others. In her spare time, Cynthia

knits, paints, dabbles in mixed media art, and loves to kickbox. Numerous books and magazines have featured Cynthia's art and photography work: she is the author of *Stash Happy Patchwork* (Lark, 2011), *Stash Happy Appliqué* (Lark, 2012) and co-author of *Serge It* (Lark, 2014). Cynthia lives with her husband Scott, sons Corry and Cameron, and pups in Southern California.

cynthiashaffer.typepad.com

cynthiashaffer.com

RUTH SINGER

Ruth is a British textile artist and designer-maker. She creates fashion and home accessories for books and magazines alongside making historically-inspired art textile pieces that are exhibited in galleries. She trained in textile history and specializes in traditional hand-worked techniques and manipulation such as Trapunto quilting and pleating. She also writes sewing books including *The Sewing Bible* and *Fabric Manipulation*. Ruth also runs a sewing school in her hometown and she teaches internationally. .

www.ruthsinger.com.

HEATHER VALENTINE

Heather is the creative juice behind The Sewing Loft, a sewing community focused on inspiring you to reclaim your creativity, one stitch at a time. After earning a degree in fashion design and pattern making from New York's Fashion Institute of Technology, Heather designed for some of the top name brands in the apparel industry. These days you can find this self-proclaimed fabric hoarder stitching the night away and dreaming of a better way to keep her thread collection detangled.

thesewingloft.com

NICOLE VOS VAN AVEZATHE

Nicole lives in Rotterdam, Netherlands with her husband, two children, and two cats. Under the name Follow the White Bunny, she makes embroidery and craft designs that are often sweet, sometimes odd, and always unique! Most of her patterns feature animals and seem to reflect a glimpse of a story, more like an illustration. She also likes to give traditional concepts, like embroidery samplers, a contemporary twist. She, for example, made a very popular Princess & the Pea embroidery sampler. Nicole hopes that her patterns will challenge people to try new stitches and techniques.

shop.followthewhitebunny.com
blog.followthewhitebunny.com

KATHLEEN WALCK

Prior to motherhood, Kathleen worked as an art teacher, museum educator, and artist. She currently strives to live creatively every day, whether through knitting, cooking, crafting, or by simply amusing her two sons in waiting rooms. She writes the blog, Katydid and Kid.

www.katydidandkid.com

JULIE ZAICHUK-RYAN

A needlecrafter with an insatiable appetite for thread, fabric, and yarn, Julie embroiders, knits, sews, makes lace, and will try to stitch down anything put in front of her. Julie loves vintage style, traditional needlework techniques, and learning about the history of crafting. She and her mother design embroidery patterns as a team called Little Dorrit & Co., and Julie self-publishes knitting and other craft patterns via her blog, Button, button.

button-button.co.uk

ACKNOWLEDGMENTS

Thank you to all the special people who made *Fat Quarters* so unique and inspiring.

To the designers for your fun and ingenious ideas
To Cynthia Shaffer for your lovely photos.
To Sue Havens for your delightful illustrations.
To the wonderful models:
    Monica Mouet
    Amina Suljic
    Camille Tiberghien
    Ella Furry
    Olivia Furry
    Cameron Shaffer
    Tiffany Jo Curtis

CREDITS

Photographer:
Cynthia Shaffer

Illustrator:
Sue Havens

Editors:
Amanda Carestio, Jill Jarnow, and Deborah Stack

Production Editor:
Kimberly Broderick

Cover Designers:
Patrice Kaplan and Igor Satanovsky

Interior Designer:
Christine Heun

Technical Copyeditor:
Kathy Brock

Copyeditor:
Gwen Kwo

Proofreader:
Claire New

INDEX

NOTE: Page numbers in *italics* indicate projects and templates. Page numbers in **bold** indicate designer information.